B.C.

Servants of God in People's China

by KATHARINE HOCKIN

FRIENDSHIP PRESS NEW YORK

Library of Congress Catalog Card Number: 62-7861

Unless otherwise indicated, Bible quotations used in this book are from the Revised Standard Version, copyright 1946 and 1952, by the Division of Christian Education of the National Council of the Churches of Christ in the United States of America.

PRINTED IN THE UNITED STATES OF AMERICA

Contents

Perspective

The dilemma of alienation forms the heart of this study. How did so deep and vast a separation come between us, Western and Chinese Christians, who had long been colleagues in a common faith? Political demarcations have fallen right across that Christian community, and the tensions of the hot war in Korea and the subsequent cold war have become the lines that now separate the articulate, patriotic segment of the Chinese church from ourselves. Politics have become more effective in their claim for divided loyalty than our faith is to unite us. As Western Christians our motives are misrepresented there, and their Christian integrity is suspect here. And on each side there is bitterness.

It would be simple to end the matter here, as many do, declaring that the Chinese church is at fault. Has it not betrayed our genuine friendship and interest and compromised its own integrity by its willing co-operation with a Communist government?

But what of our faith? Have we not also compromised the gospel? Can we escape from the responsibility of the knowledge that all those who strive to serve Jesus Christ are "members one of another" in his Body? Do we have the faith—mocked by the Communist—that the saving power of the incarnate Lord is effective, that he does not leave his people because the missionary has had to withdraw or because a

Communist government has been established, but that he has power to raise up his servants who forward his causes? Must we not act now in our faith that the Holy Spirit rules over this one world in which we must all, perhaps most uncomfortably, live together?

The dilemma of alienation and separation is most marked in relation to the more progressive and patriotic segments of the Protestant church in China. It is largely with these segments that the leaders and members of the Student Christian Movement have found their lot. Thus the following pages deal almost entirely with that part of the Chinese church which moved into this new focus of patriotism.[1] What has the coming of the People's Republic meant to them? How is it that a large group of sincere and able Chinese Christian leaders accepted the new structures affirmatively and continue to do so?

Perhaps we should remind ourselves at the outset that the search for understanding is not primarily directed to a decision about whether the Chinese Christian is wrong or right. We will not necessarily find ourselves in agreement with our Chinese fellow Christians. We may have to recognize tearing differences, but at least we may come to some glimmer of sympathetic awareness of their position. We may even feel that in such a place our actions and attitudes might be quite similar. Further, this pursuit for understanding may help us see our own involvement in the broken relation. The Apostle Paul wrote of speaking the truth in love as a characteristic of the Christian community. Perhaps we may gain the right to speak the truth in this spirit, because we shall have exposed ourselves to hearing a part of it, even when what we hear is throbbing with hurt and bitterness. For surely one must listen, and listen, and listen with loving intent to understand, to see our own failures, rather than to engage in the polemics of justification of self and condemnation of others.

[1] Notes will be found on page 125.

The author's approach is very much affected by the experience of living through the days of the revolution in West China, of seeing a change come about that was not limited to government structure, but which molded and continues to shape minds and hearts. In those early days we from the West, missionaries along with our governments, were regarded as imperialists and came to embody for many Chinese all the evils of external oppression. It was a salutary experience to find oneself not just a second-class citizen but something of an outcast, a category about which one could do nothing at all—it was just one's national origin and the color of one's skin that were to blame. For a year my work was suspended as "enemy aliens" became an embarrassment to the church. There was delay in securing an exit visa from the foreign office since I had been accused as "an international and cultural spy," though the charge was eventually dropped. During the two years that I remained in the "New China," there was an opportunity to try to understand the changing attitude of Chinese Christian friends and colleagues. Was it not worth the effort to try to see with their eyes and hear with their ears, even partially?

Some who read this book and know China will feel sad that it misrepresents what they feel to be the situation of privation and denial of freedom for the Chinese people. Others will feel it does not go far enough in recognition of the achievements of the Communist government. And because each cares so passionately, the partiality of another's interpretation is a greater offense.

Each of us in China became known for our attitudes to the new regime. In a strange way, common to eras of revolutionary pressure, we drew to ourselves the friends and information which the particular magnet of our approach and attitude invited. So the objective student of China today must take all the evidence into account, even what seems to be completely contradictory: the terrible experiences of the refugees, the testimonies of the most loyal and enthusiastic cadres, the reports by Roman Catholic priests and nuns of genuine suffering, and the patriotic statements of the Christian who holds what might be called very "progressive" political ideas indeed! Negative and positive statements do not cancel each other out in this context but are part of the whole picture. Some of the anomalies may fall into place with perspectives of more information; others will remain a puzzle.

As a Christian I believe that God Almighty is Lord of history, and that it is in history that we are called upon to discover our obedience to his will. I believe that in the events of this century the Western nations are under judgment, and that we who have sown the wind now reap—and will continue to reap—the whirlwind. I believe that God judges all who misuse power, and that for all of us there is his mercy and his grace. Many in the Chinese church see God's action in the revolutionary changes in their country, and respond in these terms to what they feel to be his call to witness in their place.

The new regime that has come to China under the aegis of the Communist Party in the People's Republic of China is a very significant development, perhaps the most important change that has come to this great nation in two thousand years, and a fact of political reality with which the rest of the world must come to terms.

We shall discover both discontinuity and continuity in the revolution of 1949. Perhaps the revolution did not have to be Communist, but the fact is that it was, and history helps us understand why this was so. For the Christian, as well as for the political statesman, there are evident lessons to be learned which, if neglected, will lead to a repetition of the badly mastered technique in other parts of the world. This is my view, one which has been molded by both experience and study, and with the tempering of concern to understand those with whom I worked and in whose Christian integrity and sincerity I had come to believe as much as in my own. But our discussion is essentially open ended. Let the reader consider and accept the challenge to struggle for understanding and then come to his own working conclusions, with a willingness, shared by the author, to modify, to change, and to grow.

A word should be said about the use of terms. "The People's Republic of China" is the name under which the new regime was proclaimed in 1949, and it is probably the one that will be used by Chinese for some time to come. This formal title and the shorter "People's China" may serve to bring us closer to an understanding of the casual attitudes of the ordinary Chinese than does the more common designation of "Red" or "Communist." While these terms may be quite acceptable in China, for us they tend to be emotionally charged and may thus lead to distortion.

In the early period of the People's Republic the term "liberation" became current in referring to the political change that had brought the Communists to power. One soon ceased to be troubled by connotations of "freedom" or of "bondage" and slipped into the usage of the day, the matter-of-fact vocabulary of ordinary communication.

A Chinese from Hong Kong who is far from sympathetic to the characteristics of communism said to me, "Everyone knows what you mean when you say 'before liberation' or refer to 'People's China.' " Similarly for current clarity we may speak of the "People's Liberation Army" and the "People's government."

One of the tragic tendencies of a world like ours, where power and ideological blocs form, is that we tend to become more and more rigidly polarized. Refugees moving in both directions strengthen the antagonism, and each side becomes less tolerant of deviation, demanding its own type of conformity. Opposition voices that may ideally bring wholeness to a self-critical society tend to be eliminated both in the free West and the totalitarian East.

When I started on the project of writing this book, I expressed a desire to write "with my Chinese friends over my shoulder." Much that is included in this manuscript has been sharpened or clarified by past conversations that sent me searching into history and moved me forward in the quest for a larger perspective. The telling of this background story has on many occasions brought a positive response from many Chinese students in North America who have recognized with appreciation the attempt to be objective. I have tried to prove faithful to the friendship of Chinese Christians who, when the Communist armies were on the horizon, had their own strong views. So up to that point I speak out of the sharing and comradeship that once were richly fruitful in glimpsing, at least fragmentarily, what it may mean to look at the world from an Asian viewpoint. This is not spoken with intent to be arrogant but simply to say that the Asian is not the North American. Even within the wide range of Asian approaches today, there is a common base which is clearly *not* that of either Canada or the United States.

For the discussion of what is taking place now in the Christian community in China, it is impossible to be aware of one's friends at one's shoulder. They have long since been unwilling to remain in such a position. The reading and study that have gone into the preparation of this book have brought home the vast alienation that now separates us.

The reader must share in the struggle to make sense of what is happening today and why we, Chinese and Americans who are Christians and have been friends, now find ourselves so very, very far apart. He must wrestle with the real issues, for the author does not have the answer to the essential problem of a divided and broken Christian fellowship. The assignment that has involved writing this study has left me more perplexed than before. So this presentation is in truth open ended. The reader must discover the way forward himself in God's work of reconciliation!

1 · Contemporary Glimpses of People's China

HONG KONG VERSUS CANTON

A letter from a Hong Kong businessman, a Chinese Christian and a graduate of Lingnan University, compares what he saw in Kwangtung Province on a visit there in May, 1960, with life in Hong Kong:

Hong Kong good points: A busy market, with plenty of goods; freedom of thought, of action, of speech, and of residence; a place where money can do anything, where individuality can exist and where the law protects individual life and property.

Hong Kong bad points: The poor are getting poorer and the rich richer; the power of money fosters covetousness, and this confuses the sense of justice; the laws can be manipulated by the rich and powerful to uphold injustice, and thus the ignorant people still live under exploitation. Bureaucratism prevails; the system is nominally democratic, but actually is loaded in favor of the privileged classes. Humane feelings are thin as paper; poverty is despised more than prostitution is. The over-development of individualism creates a selfish spirit and a disregard of the needs of others.

Canton good points: A peaceful social order, with no thievery; doors need not be locked at night; police are not needed, for the people themselves keep order. Everything is for the public; there is no private property. A spirit of humility prevails, with no striving for first place. Gambling and vice have been swept away. Everyone is working for productive purposes, to help the country and not for oneself. There is universal education.

Canton bad points: The market place is idle, there are no goods for sale. There is no freedom of thought, of speech, of action or of residence. Every act must be reported to the police. Even if you have money you can't buy food; it's as if money were useless. No individuality is allowed, thus making men like cattle and horses. People work too hard and yet are neither warmed nor fed, to the detriment of their health. Communists act as though they thought ordinary people had superhuman strength; they starve people's bodies and tax their strength, driving them mercilessly. It is a system of hate, with no love in it.[1]

The letter concludes with the comment that each system has its good and bad points, and voices a wistful hope that a system might be devised that could combine the good points of both.

* * *

What is happening in China today? How much change has really been wrought by the new regime? We hear something of the famine that seems to have haunted the land. Is the lessening of the number of invited visitors due to the food situation or to a more basic withdrawal of China into her own life again? The refugee stream continues into Hong Kong. There seem to be differences between Peking and Moscow. The commune as a structure seems to have been modified. Our news only adds up to a confused picture, so that it is difficult to arrive at anything that might even approximate an accurate image of contemporary China.

Our newspapers and magazines have easy access to the reports of the refugee and the exile, and these are part of the story. Occasionally one reads of a visitor who has been naïvely impressed with what he has seen in a brief visit. There have been a few Christian delegations and some individual Christians who have been entertained by the People's Republic and have been able to converse with Chinese Christian leaders and share in the worship of the churches of that country.

The following account of a visit to China is presented as

one of the most recent. The writer, Mrs. Nancy H. Lapwood, was previously a missionary and a missionary's daughter, so she possesses a long perspective from which to appraise the present situation.[2]

CHINA REVISITED[3]

. . . We travelled extensively in China, saw a great deal, talked with the ordinary people wherever we went, took Kodachrome pictures very freely (bringing them all back to England to be developed) and received a most heart-warming welcome from our many old friends, Christian and non-Christian alike. We were treated with the utmost courtesy and cordiality and felt very much at home.

Our hosts wished to show us their rolling-mills and their motor-works, their dams and their bridges, their blast-furnaces and their tractor factories; all of these were impressive against the background of the old China. Factories raising their tall chimneys in the middle of the fields didn't fill me with undiluted joy, but they were, to the Chinese, symbols of their advance from a backward, semi-feudal, semi-colonial nation exploited by more powerful, industrialized countries, to a modern, independent, industrialized state with a rising standard of living for all.

Many people in the West are prepared to concede that China is now making great strides in her effort to catch up with the more advanced industrial areas of the world. Then they shake their heads and add, "But at what a cost in human suffering!" I therefore determined to concentrate most of my energy on observing the *people*—in their homes, factories, workshops, fields, communes, schools, kindergartens, and hospitals. Again I tried to see China through *their* eyes, in the context of *their* "frame of reference." Here briefly are my main impressions.

The over-all standard of living was slowly but definitely rising, though it was still far below that of most Western nations. The children looked well-fed and bonny, even in the old, overcrowded slums of Shanghai and Wuhan. The young people seemed on the average taller than formerly, with physique greatly improved through regular physical exercise, and, in the case of students, through their participation in manual labour in fields and vegetable gardens. Rationing was already stringent in the summer of 1960, a "disaster" year, although our hosts, through pride or politeness, tried to hide it from us. We heard, for instance, that the minimum meat ration in Peking was four ounces per person per month. Rations were graded according to the amount of physical labour undertaken by each person, with special priorities for children, nursing mothers, the sick and the old. The remarkable thing was that everyone looked so fit. Those of our close friends whose standard of living used to be above the average now accept what they call "voluntary Puritan austerity," that all may have enough of the basic necessities. We saw no one in rags and very few in patched clothing. Clothes were, in general, simple, colourful and clean.

Health and physical fitness for all was the obvious aim. Beautiful new hospitals were springing up in large cities; older ones, often founded by missionary societies, were being enlarged to cope with more patients. The one built in Tientsin under my father's leadership was specializing in bone and tumour cases and was claimed to be doing as many operations for T.B. of the spine as any other hospital in the world. The major cities always had fairly adequate medical facilities, but now small towns and villages have their simple but well-equipped hospitals, clinics and health centres.

Sports stadiums, swimming-pools and basketball fields can be seen not only in Peking and Shanghai, but in remote country areas as well. . . .

Primary education is now available for all children, but high schools, technical colleges and universities cannot yet fill the steadily growing demand for higher education. Everywhere we went we saw groups of factory workers, housewives and peasants engaged in literacy classes during the lunch hour. The Latin alphabet is being taught in kindergarten and primary classes as a help to learning the very difficult Chinese ideographs, but not as a substitute for that very ancient and beautiful written language. Knowledge of 2,000 characters is still needed for the reading of a daily newspaper. It has been claimed that education and literacy are nothing but tools by which the Communist leaders can indoctrinate their people. It is true that all information reaching the Chinese people through press, books, radio or television is channelled through or vetoed by the party organization, and the people as a whole are very ill-informed as to the real attitudes of people in the West. But popular education is much more than just a means of learning of the policies of their government. It opens up a whole new world of literature and science formerly closed to more than half the Chinese people. It also provides a means of expression and creative writing for the formerly inarticulate.

With all this obvious material advance in China, it was easy to see why our friends claimed they now had a government which really cared for everybody. But it was interesting to see that this did not make them feel individually unimportant, dependent on the government for direction and support, a mere cog in a vast machine. Everyone, from the child in the nursery school to the old man in the commune "Home of Respect for the Aged," felt his contribution was significant and took a pride in doing things "better, quicker, more thoroughly and with less waste" than ever before. The government leaders have certainly been skilful in their use of catchy slogans and the ideas carefully implanted in the minds of the ordinary people through their "small discussion groups," but they have been the means of arousing popular enthusiasm without which many of the vast projects now being undertaken by the people would have had to wait for state action. . . .

Virtually all Western missionaries have left China, but the Chinese Christian church continues. Christians form a tiny minority of the population (less than half of one per cent), but along with the other religious and minority groups, they have special representation in the All-China Congress (Parliament). They are guaranteed religious freedom under their constitution and their churches are free from taxes if used entirely for religious purposes.

Joan and I attended two church services in Peking. The congregations numbered 75 on each occasion, with the young, the middle-aged and the elderly in roughly equal proportions. In the Community Church, Shanghai, we joined a congregation of 450 which seemed a fair cross-section of the community, but with the young outnumbering the old. The singing of hymns from the *"Pu T'ien Sung Tsan,"* a very good collection published more than 20 years ago, was vigorous and tuneful. Sermons were a straight-forward expounding of Christian teaching.

Bibles continue to be published in China and are sold in considerable numbers. There are two large Protestant theological seminaries at Peking and Nanking, both union institutions formed by the amalgamation of a number of smaller theological colleges founded by the different denominations. Full church union has not yet come in China, but denominational differences are less and less important. Joint services are held in most Protestant churches every Sunday, instead of only at major church festivals as in the past. Chinese Christians insist that their freedom to believe and to preach the gospel is a fact, and they feel deeply hurt when Christians in the West say it is not.

But it is certainly not easy to be a Christian in China today. The Christian finds himself in the midst of a successful Communist revolution, being told on every hand that all religion is superstitious nonsense and not necessary in this scientific age. Moreover he is reminded by his neighbors and workmates that Christianity came by way of the West, that missionaries came into China "behind the gunboats," benefitted by the extra-territoriality forced on a weak China by the "Unequal Treaties." For Muslims and Buddhists there is little or no conflict between their religious and their patriotic loyalties. But the Christians must prove themselves patriotic Chinese citizens. The more highly educated among them declare that, in the past, they were too often divorced from the sufferings of the ordinary people of China, occupying a position of prestige and privilege, with chances of higher education and study abroad, beyond the reach of most of their fellow-countrymen. Now they feel impelled to repudiate social and political ideas unconsciously incorporated into the teaching of many of the missionaries; to return to the teaching of Jesus and the experience of the early church for their own inward renewal; to reinterpret Christianity in Chinese terms and in the context of a rapidly changing, revolutionary state. Not only do they see it as reprehensible to live by exploiting others, they even feel it morally wrong to be rich when those about them are poor. So they have come to accept socialism as more Christian than capitalism.

2 · *The Lord of History and His Servants*

" 'What do you think? A man had two sons; and he went to the first and said, "Son, go and work in the vineyard today." And he answered, "I will not"; but afterward he repented and went. And he went to the second and said the same; and he answered, "I go, sir," but did not go. Which of the two did the will of the father?' " (Matt. 21:28-31)

* * *

"You know," said the Chinese teacher, with a bitter sigh, "it is really true that the Communist Party has done more for my country in a year than the Christians did in the last century." It was 1951, and for a year we had been under the military administration of the new regime, which had proclaimed the People's Republic of China in Peking on October 1, 1949. There followed a discussion of the relative effectiveness of hate and love as motivating forces to national advancement, a discussion that might well have deteriorated into an argument had it not been for the respect and affection that firmly undergirded the relationship between the Chinese Christian woman and myself, a Canadian missionary. It was hard to understand how my Chinese friend could see so much that was affirmative in the new China, but she was a person of integrity, of sincere devotion to the well-being of her people, and also one who treasured the friendship of many of us who were foreigners.

This conversation was part of a struggling quest for understanding. There were growing differences between us. She was Chinese, and deep in her spirit were the barbs of insult and indignity that all Chinese feel when they think of the history of Asian relations with Western nations.

There was also the immediate difference in point of view. She knew that whatever China's future was to be, she must be part of it. I, a foreigner, had the alternative of leaving the country. This alternative became realistically the only choice later on when China joined the cause of North Korea, making me an "enemy alien." She had already been drawn into her university discussion group for political study. As a woman with valuable professional skills needed by the new country, she was brought into the constructive activities of the Women's Federation. I was isolated from all this, for I was automatically classed as an antirevolutionary, especially after the outbreak of the Korean War when all North Americans were enemy aliens. So the colleagueship and affection we had shared was under strain.

My Chinese friend, looking at such accomplishments of the new order as stable government, the reconstruction already achieved, and the promise of more benefits for all the people of China, had concluded that the leadership of the Communist Party was justified in many of its claims to be serving the people. And one was reminded of the parable of the two sons, both with their sinful shortcomings, the one who agreed to obey and did nothing, and the other who refused but changed his mind. There seemed no doubt in the mind of speaker or hearer which of the two carried out the father's purpose.

Basic to the quest for understanding is our own approach to the world in which we as Christians live. What are our convictions about the way God works in history? Can we clarify our attitudes here? The Biblical record remains a common heritage for all Christians behind whatever curtain they live in this twentieth century, be it iron, bamboo, or velvet. We must also remind ourselves of the fact that there are historical roots to the situations of our day.

We are generally so partially informed on Asian history that we are ill-equipped to see events in their agelong perspective, with the inevitability of cause and effect. We tend to interpret present happenings only as they affect us today. The Asian is very conscious of his own rich heritage, so our ignorance is itself a barrier to good relationships.

Christian belief is grounded in the doctrine of God as creator of the world, the ordainer of the order in which his creature, man, lives with the gift of free will. We believe that God, the Father of our Lord Jesus Christ, continues to act in ongoing rhythms of mercy and judgment which we see throughout the Biblical record.

Four concepts in the Bible regarding the role of the state and the attitude of the believer are important for our purposes here, as each illustrates a contemporary Christian judgment on the Communist state.

For the Old Testament prophet, God is Lord of historic events. The political acumen of Isaiah of Jerusalem is grounded in his statesmanlike perception of God's governance. He saw the mounting power of Assyria in theocentric terms. The chosen people had turned from the obedient service of their God, and under the lordship of a *caring,* not just a vengeful Lord, judgment had to come. "Ah, Assyria, the rod of my anger, the staff of my fury! Against a godless nation I send him, and against the people of my wrath I command him." (Is. 10:5, 6) This does not mean that these alien nations are merely instruments of God's anger. They too are responsible for their apostasy and will in their turn fall under judgment, but Israel need not escape into self-righteous comfort on this account. Her own responsibility is that of obedience. So the disobedience of the son who claims his sonship is countered by the obedience of the other son who partially fulfils God's will even though not acknowledging his sovereignty.

Here we see the state as inescapably under God's direction and judgment. The unfortunate events of the late forties in China, the increased corruption of the Kuomintang government, and the failures of Western diplomacy to bring about a coalition between Chinese parties led to the renewed hostilities of civil war in China. It was easy for even the Western Christian to see the relevance of this prophetic judgment on a government that had failed its people.

In the Biblical record the alien ruler emerges also in a more positive light, in the role played by Persian kings in the rebuilding of Jerusalem. Cyrus is spoken of as the "anointed" of God. " 'He is my shepherd, and he shall fulfill all my purpose.' " (Is. 44:28, *cf.* 45:1) Here the obedience of the unbeliever is even more marked, for it is the heathen Cyrus and his heirs who encourage the exiles to return to their own place and to restore worship in Jerusalem. It is difficult for the Western Christian to see any similarity between Cyrus, the shepherd, and the conditioned tolerance of the Chinese Communist Party to religious groups. But the basis of this approach underlies the following document by Y. T. Wu, a Christian leader who early supported the new Chinese regime.

> In New China the people have aroused themselves; in the material and intellectual reconstruction wonderful new improvements in the life of the common man are being seen every day, and yet many of us Christians look upon these things with pessimism, doubt, or even antagonism. Many believers are still absorbed in the preaching of the Last Day, and of the misery of human life. But both Christians and non-Christians are citizens of the New China; should the benefit of the many bring sorrow to the few? When God is in this new time bringing such benefits to those who do not believe on Him, will He at the same time cast away His own people? No, the trouble is not in God, nor in these new things, but in our failure to understand them or in willfully understanding them amiss. . . .[1]

Do not dismiss this statement too lightly. Its writer is well versed in both Scripture and theology and must be listened to seriously, for he speaks for a significant group of Chinese Christians, with whose attitude we may have to disagree, but who remain part of the Body of Christ, and who also remain within Communist China, faithful in the terms of their own understanding to the name of Christian. Is our faithfulness any greater, even in our own terms? For us both, unequivocally, God is Lord of history and event.

In the New Testament there is much that might be discussed. There is the cryptic recognition, in our Lord's parable of the coin, that there is a realm where Caesar must be given his rights along with the human responsibility to recognize the sovereignty of God. Very pertinent in the life of the Christian today is the admonition of Paul in Romans 13 to his contemporaries, where he speaks of co-operation with the civil authorities, and the obligation to pay taxes and fulfil the duties of the citizen.

It is interesting to note these passages over against the fourth Biblical picture of the state in the familiar Revelation description of the beast (see Rev. 13). It is helpful to remember that the situation under which the book of Revelation was written was one of the most corrupt, decadent, and cruel periods of the Roman Empire, with a Caesar who was intent on making himself God. It is common for us to make a too simple equation of communism with the anti-Christ, because of the open atheism of Communist humanism, and this may blind us to the functional atheism that may be found much closer to home. Here again may we listen to our fellow Christians who must carry on the witness in their own lands.[2] For them the Communist cannot be dismissed as anti-Christ but must be approached as a "brother for whom Christ died." Is this not also true for us? They also face the political choice of accepting and working within their situation in order to maintain the very life of the church and to carry on the Christian witness. Let us not simplify this to a stark black-and-white choice. Just as the alternatives for us are not clear in every matter on which Christians must take a stand, so there are many shades of gray in the political stands that Chinese Christians take. And we must remember that political expediency is not only to be found in Christian circles other than our own. Is it absurd to recognize that they, our Christian brothers, see the same fault in us? They term us "imperialist." We taunt them with collaboration and betraying compromise. If we leave the relationship here, what of the Kingdom?

Here, then, are four aspects of the Biblical concept of the state. 1. It is under judgment. 2. It may be a permissive agent for reconstruction. 3. It provides the framework for civil life and order, though at times it may deny human and spiritual values. 4. God is sovereign over the state, whether acknowledged or not, and Christ is Lord. Our task as Christians in the context of this study is fundamentally the quest for obedience. How can we be faithful servants? We often ask, "How can we get ahead of communism?" or "Why does God allow all this evil to happen?" Should not our question be, "What is God saying to us through the events of our day? And what then should be our obedient response?"

Our common obedience! What does this mean? Each reader must answer for himself. We affirm that God is Lord of history. Let us also be reminded of the central doctrine of Christian experience, that of the incarnation—God in Christ reconciling the world to himself. These are such familiar and comforting words. But the methodology of the incarnation was not soft or easy. There was the steel of suffering and the fiber of acceptance of the costly burden of sin. When Jesus spoke the beatitude about the peacemakers and their blessedness, was all this in his mind? "Blessed are the peacemakers, for they shall be called sons of God." What was the lot of the Son of God? If we feel that an ideology such as communism is simply the anti-Christ, then it is fairly simple to see the Christian's lot as martyrdom. If we see a more fundamental historical judgment, then the task of the incarnate Christ reconciling the world is much more complicated and difficult. The dimensions of the witness of reconciliation in this mid-twentieth century world challenge all servants of God who confess his name to a costly stretching of our understanding. A Chinese Christian leader, in one of the rare opportunities for conversation since the establishment of the People's Republic of China, spoke to a group in Europe with the plea, "Please don't pray *at* us. Don't even pray *for* us. Pray *with* us." And Dr. Walter Freytag wrote in 1957, after spending a period as a visiting lecturer in a Chinese theological college:

> As I met, on my last evening in China, with a little group of Chinese pastors who for special reasons, were particularly close to me, I said to them after a long and frank discussion: "You know that you are being prayed for. And many will expect me to tell them when I get home, for what they should pray when they think of you." Without hesitation came but one answer: "That the Gospel shall grow in China!"[3]

* * *

A Chinese Christian treatise on Church and State appeared in the August, 1957, issue of the *Nanking Seminary Magazine*. The author, Kiang Wen-han, is one of the General Secretaries of the Young Men's Christian Association of China, was a leader in the World Student Christian Federation, and was a Chinese visitor to North American Student Christian conferences on several occasions. The following summary is quoted from the *China Bulletin*.

> The main body of the article is divided into three sections: 1. The Point of View of Western Christians; 2. The Recognition by Chinese Christians of New China; and 3. The Biblical View.
>
> 1. In the first section he begins with a brief review of the history of Church and state relations in the West, from the Emperor

Constantine down. On coming to the present he concludes that there is no real distinction between national and free churches, as we see them in Europe and America, for in spite of the formal separation of church and state in some countries, "actually the church is at the service of capitalism, and so what we see is merely a convenient division of labor between church and state."

He goes on to refer with evident approval to the struggle of Western Christians against totalitarian forms of government, objecting only to the fact that they "indiscriminately include the Soviet Union along with Germany and Italy," and indeed date the beginning of modern totalitarianism from the October Revolution in 1917. "They were not able to deny the economic achievements of the socialist nations, but they maintained that totalitarianism meant the end of human freedom, that the abolition of private property put men in slavery to their governments, because private property is the necessary condition of human freedom. They admitted that private property created classes in society, but they maintained that arbitrary government also created its own new class system."

This section concludes with an approving reference to the fundamental theological questions which Western Christians have raised. First, what is the basis of governmental authority? On this he quotes with commendation the position of Niebuhr on whether a government is divine or demonic. "When a government tries to encompass all of human life, making itself into God, it is then demonic." Secondly, where is the Christian's ultimate loyalty? In discussing this question he recognizes the possibility of an unavoidable conflict.

2. In the second section he reiterates what is now the conventional view in China, that the missionaries were made use of by imperialism with the result that until the coming of Communism, the Christian church in China was either consciously or unconsciously subservient to reactionary government. Since then the situation has changed. "Chinese Christians have come to recognize that the People's Government under the leadership of the Chinese Communist Party is sincere in its policy of freedom of religious belief, and is willing to help the Church in any difficulties it may meet. Since both the standard of living and the level of public morals have been steadily rising, we feel that there are improved conditions for proclaiming the Gospel in New China, and that therefore to participate in the government is one way to bear witness for the Lord. . . . Although we and

the Communists differ in faith, we are all Chinese, and are one in our desire for the increasing prosperity and glory of our country. This difference in belief is therefore no hindrance to intimate cooperation in the building up of our country."

. . . .

In fact, he says, Western concern at this point is only an expression of Western prejudice. "Western Christians have a deep prejudice against anyone who supports Communism, and consider that such a person cannot be a true Christian. Is not this surprising? Can Christianity only survive in a capitalistic society?"

3. The last section is on the Biblical View. He notes that the Bible is not very explicit on the question of the relation of Church and State, but still it is possible to infer a Christian attitude from the teaching of Christ and the apostles. Although Christ recognized that in general His kingdom was not of this world, still he loved his own country and wept over it, and was concerned enough to enunciate a deep truth in His "Render unto Caesar" saying. "It teaches that though there are some things which do indeed belong to Caesar, still Caesar is not everything, and Caesar is not God." Paul in general had a favorable attitude toward the government, but Peter could boldly say, "We must obey God rather than men," and the book of Revelation describes Rome as "drunk with the blood of the saints and the witnesses of Jesus."

From all of this he draws the conclusion: "The attitude of the church towards the state depends upon the nature of the government concerned. . . . We must obey a government that serves the people and resist one that does not. And in each case what we do is a witness for the Lord." And according to his experience, the People's Government has the proper qualifications, because it both serves the people and guarantees freedom of religious belief. "We are faithful to the God revealed by Christ, and do not feel any inconsistency between this and our love for our country. Our church has now established its own independence, and is therefore in a position to enter into fuller relations with the churches in other countries. We believe that there is a bright future for the church in New China, because we are convinced that the future is in the hands of Almighty God."[4]

3 · *Imperial China*

"When a ruler treats his subjects like grass and dirt, Then the subjects treat him as a bandit and an enemy."
Mencius, fourth century B.C.

"The people are the sea and the ruler is the boat; the sea can support the boat, but it can also sink it."
Hsun Tzu, second century A.D.

"By winning the support of the people, the kingdom is won; by losing the support of the people, the kingdom is lost."
Commentary on the Great Learning, eighth century A.D.

FEUDAL DECADENCE

There had to be a revolution in China. The internal breakdown of Chinese feudal society and the pressures of foreign encroachment taking advantage of the weaknesses within have been determinative in the birth of contemporary China.

Under the ancient feudal system, the fields remained common land and were granted to the peasants for cultivation but were not owned by individuals. As the feudal system crumbled, the fields came to be bought and sold. The landowning class emerged as the power group that really controlled most aspects of the common life.

Eventually too the scholars, the old literati who were the administrators and civil servants also came from the landed strata of society, as they were the only persons who had leisure for study. There was a close relationship between Confucian scholarship and political appointment, for from the imperial examinations (on Confucian teachings), the leading government personnel were chosen. This further strengthened the hold of the privileged landlord classes.

Sometimes discontent burst into flame, but these periodic rebellions did not change the structure of society. For within the classic tradition there was a rationale for the overthrowing of the ruler, traceable to a Mencian concept of the "sacred right of rebellion." When the Son of Heaven, the dynastic ruler, showed that he had lost the Mandate of Heaven through his evident misrule, then revolt was in order. So dynasties fell, but the system continued.

The nineteenth century, however, was to see a new combination of forces as the impact of an expanding and self-confident Western world began to press on the Manchu Dynasty. Eventually the peasantry was to find it possible to throw off the burden of centuries, a process completed when the economic hold of the landlord was broken in the final act of land reform under the People's Government in 1950.

Most of us foreigners who lived in China were settled in cities. While we were aware of the hard lot of the peasant and of the blocks to rural redevelopment, we were not fully cognizant of the extent of abuse possible under the system which put the villages, the countryside, and its ordinary folk so completely in the power of the landowner. Peasant unrest may be seen as a barometer of the breakdown of the feudal structure of the old China, of the dynastic decay as the Manchu rulers lost their hold on the nation, and as corruption, jockeyings for power, and internal dissolution took effect.

FOREIGN IMPERIALISM

The other major strand of discontent came from the relations with the Western world through the period which has been called "The Hundred Years of Unequal Treaties." The late eighteenth and early nineteenth centuries marked the outreach of European adventurers in discovery and for the profits of trade and commerce. Government interests and missionary activity followed. We are familiar with the rationale of the white man's burden and our general Western superiority assumptions.

What was not recognized in this initial encounter was the native pride of the Chinese people, rooted in an ancient history and a self-satisfied culture that had since time immemorial looked on all outside China as untutored barbarians. China was the Middle Kingdom, the mid-point between heaven and the nether spheres, between east and west, between north and south. Here all was centered; in cultural attainment, human relations, art, music, and all refinement, the Middle Kingdom was perfection.

The northern deserts and steppes, where the isolationist, self-content China built her Great Wall, the Himalayan plateau, and the eastern seas were all effective in keeping China to herself. So she lived, not only in contentment but in self-satisfaction, born of the assurance of her own central position in the civilized world.

Here then is the pride of China, a pride that has been deeply affronted for the last century and more by the brash superiorities of the West, and which continues to be affronted by much of our unconscious dismissal of Asian peoples today. Pride affronted grows into bitterness and hatred —venomous in its expression—and seems to inspire resentment and hurt in response. And so relationships deteriorate. Historically China always regarded herself as what, in fact, she was—a truly great power with a whole group of satellite and tribute-bearing states, making an extensive empire with more continuity than any other nation in the world.

With this reminder, perhaps we are ready to see some of the significant by-products in attitude and relationship which were built up into dangerous proportions through the years of foreign aggression. One should read the story of this period from 1834 on in detail.

The Opium War, 1839-1842, marked the intervention of British military power to protect the trade carried on by the British East India Company. The Chinese administration was forced not only to continue accepting shipments of opium but also to agree to the first of the unequal treaties, that of Nanking, in 1842. It was then that Hong Kong was ceded to Britain, other treaty ports opened, and a long-term foreign encroachment into territorial China began.

There followed a series of unequal treaties by which Great Britain, France, Germany, Russia, and finally the United States secured a variety of concessions which no sovereign state would surrender if it could avoid doing so. Each foreign power secured the right known as "the most favored nation clause," according to which a concession made to one of the powers was claimed as a right by each of the others without independent negotiation. If Britain secured a new foothold in a treaty port, or a new right to navigate inland waters, all other powers claimed the same right. Concessions of land under foreign administration and occupation were soon dotted all along the coast of China, with Shanghai as the major reminder of foreign occupation. Rights of extraterritoriality flouted Chinese sovereignty in her own land. China became in truth a colony, not of one nation but of many, and as such was in a sense even more fragmented and helpless, her government tottering under the once alien but now domesticated Manchu Dynasty.

It is well, at this point, to note the relation of the missionary outreach of the Christian churches to the unequal treaties. This was the period of missionary pioneering in many parts of the world, as the zeal for the evangelization of the world sent courageous witnesses to the far corners of the globe. Robert Morrison had served his patient apprenticeship in Canton and, along with others such as Dr. Peter

Parker, found the restrictions on his movement and activity under the Manchu imperial regime very crippling to an effective preaching of the gospel. It was perhaps inevitable that these servants of God should put pressures on their own governments to wrest from the Chinese authorities edicts for the toleration of Christianity and concessions to permit travel and purchase of land in the interior in order that the gospel might be preached. Both Roman Catholic and Protestant missionaries increased their activities, but they found that the official lowering of bars did not mean real welcome from the Chinese population. Christianity remained foreign to Chinese traditional thought.

The Tai-ping Rebellion of 1850-64 illustrates the interweaving of several strands. Its leader, Hung Hsiu-chuan, had come across a copy of the New Testament and, inspired by the concept of the kingdom of God, set out to bring in the day of the "heavenly kingdom of the great peace" for the suffering peasants. Was not this a legitimate goal for a servant of God? The movement for land redistribution and social reform met with some immediate success, and its Christian idealism and ethical standards appealed at first to Western interests. But when the Tai-pings threatened the international ports and foreign interests, the Ever Victorious Army, launched by three American adventurers, responded to the appeals of the Manchu government. The rebellion was thus suppressed by foreign mercenaries, citizens of Christian nations. Here surely is a tangled story of right and wrong, of idealism and self-interest, of revolutionary promise and cynical politics.

Meantime, as trade prospered, a new Chinese comprador class was developing, the predecessors of the modern capitalists. Simultaneously missionaries were responsible for the establishment of schools with a modern curriculum. The interplay of all these forces meant a yeasting within China, which continually threatened to explode.

The Boxer Rebellion in 1900 was started by a secret order, the Righteous Fists Society, hence the name "Boxer." This outbreak was basically antidynastic but was cleverly turned into antiforeign channels by the astute Empress Dowager. It was not hard to rally popular support with a cry of "drive out the foreigner." All across the land the resentments of the past boiled over into acts of violence and recrimination. More Chinese than foreigners were actually killed, for many of them were accused of being the "running dogs" of the foreigners. Many Christians met death at this time. The direct attack on foreign property and persons provided the necessary practical threat to summon troops which ended the rebellion. In the international claims settlement following the Boxer uprising, the sum of 450,000,000 *taels* ($333,000,000) was to be paid as indemnity for damages to foreign nations and organizations, over a period of thirty-nine years. To underwrite this, the revenues of the imperial maritime customs provided the security, and further claims were enforced which again affronted a proud but militarily helpless nation.[1]

At this time Protestant missionaries, individually and corporately, became aware of the unfortunate link between Christianity and foreign aggression in the Chinese mind. The collective claims of Protestant missions in the indemnity fund were scaled down to actual damage to property. Some of the major missionary groups refused to make any claims at all. Some individual missionary families put in heavy demands, however, as they were free to do. At this time the Roman Catholic churches and missions secured sizable indemnities as claims for losses which were much larger than those suffered by the Protestant groups. They were able to purchase urban and rural land holdings, a move that was to identify the hierarchy of this church particularly with the landed classes in years to come. The American government was to receive a large indemnity, but it decided to turn the fund back in scholarships for young Chinese to secure modern education in the United States. This was at the time a genuine act of generosity and enlightenment, but it was later to be interpreted as a manifestation of "cultural imperialism," a charge which, for basic appreciation of contemporary Chinese attitudes, we must try to understand.

Meantime, reform clubs and revolutionary associations continued to proliferate. The discontent with foreign aggression remained, and all combined into a very combustible situation. The immediate revolution is associated with the name of Dr. Sun Yat-sen, born of middle peasant stock, near the city of Canton. He grew up in the countryside but later was sent to Honolulu and Hong Kong, successively, for his education, helped by members of the family who had emigrated to Hawaii. Sun Yat-sen, a Christian imbued with high ideals of service to his countrymen, trained as a doctor. He became the organizer of revolutionary forces, particularly from overseas. It was not safe for him to work from a base in China.

The Republic of China was born on October 10, 1911, an anniversary since known as the Double Tenth, and Dr. Sun hurried home to be proclaimed its first president. Yuan Shih-kai, who had been in charge of imperial armies, turned from his Manchu suzerains and joined the revolutionary cause. As Yuan was a man of considerable influence, prestige, and ambition, Sun Yat-sen resigned the presidency in Yuan's favor in the hope of insuring national unity. China thus entered its new era.

* * *

The following is an excerpt from a speech by a government forestry official, Chen Ming-shu, at the Three-Self Second Anniversary Service in Wuhan on September 23, 1952, as printed in the magazine, *The New Church:*

I am a common man come to discuss with you the duties that confront the Christian church at this time. What I have to say concerns not only the Christians, but generally speaking all religious groups.

The purpose of all religion is to liberate man and lead him into the way of doing good. By his good works man is respected in society and will have much influence. Great leaders will find it difficult to exterminate him or his influence, so they will turn about and use him. He thus comes to serve the powers that exist. For that reason Marx has said that "Religion is the opiate of the people."

. . . .

The same has happened in Christianity. It was born when the masses were being oppressed by the Roman Empire. In the confusion that followed, the church became the tool of the nations. Though the latter were enemies of the church, they could not crush it. But under Charlemagne of the Franks, the church became a feudalistic power controlling the lives of men.

Now the capitalists are using the church to oppress workers and farmers, making the masses serve the bourgeoisie. They have taken Jesus' statement in Matthew 11:28 and turned it to themselves and so anesthetize the people.

The above facts are common to all countries, but in China it is different. When Christianity was brought to China, it was to an undeveloped society. Shipping increased when it was discovered that China was an untouched storehouse. Other countries began colonial aggression. They came first with obeisance and gifts for the emperors. But as they came to understand China, they changed their tactics. As Marx has said, they came from the West in armed ships,—bringing opium and Christianity. Following this aggression, many unequal treaties were entered into with the West, and China was anesthetized.

. . . .

It is true that Communism is atheistic, but they have laid hold on the history of materialism. They understand how religion came into being, and what keeps it alive, namely that man does not understand nature . . . and so is convinced that God controls it.

. . . .

You followers of Jesus Christ, who was a great revolutionist, you ought to follow in the love, justice, and equity of Jesus Christ, that the oppressed masses might be set free, that they might be blessed, and thus come to support this great victory, which is indeed reconciled to Christianity, but which far excels the teachings of Christianity.[2]

4 · *Republican China*

FRAGMENTATION, 1912-1920

From Sun Yat-sen's Will

For forty years I have devoted myself to the cause of the people's revolution with but one end in view: the elevation of China to a position of freedom and equality among the nations. My experiences during those forty years have convinced me that to attain this goal we must bring about an awakening for our own people and ally ourselves in a common struggle with those peoples of the world who treat us as equals.

The Revolution is not yet finished. Let all our comrades follow my plan for National Reconstruction and the Manifesto issued by the First National Convention of our Party, and make every effort to carry them out. Above all, my recent declarations in favor of holding a National Convention of the People of China and abolishing the unequal treaties should be carried into effect as soon as possible.

* * *

Following the period of the dynastic dissolution and the decadence of weak Manchu rule, the rebuilding of the country was an imposing task. Yuan Shih-kai did manage to hold the country together and in 1913 secured a reorganization loan from Great Britain, France, Germany, and Japan. The security for this was provided by income from the salt tax, held as a government monopoly. Foreign personnel took over the collection of this tax and appointed Western officials who lived in inland cities near centers of salt production. The facts that each ounce of salt was taxed and that all Chinese need this ingredient as an essential for their frugal diet were thus literally salt in the wound of discontent and resentment against the foreigner. The common man was ignorant of the reason for the tax, but he knew it was an alien burden.

For the missionary there was a new sense of corporate endeavor as the numbers of Chinese Christians multiplied slowly and as such people saw the service of God and the reconstruction of their country as challenging all their creativity. It could also be said that the building up of the country was really undertaken in the service of God, as the Chinese Christian patriots espoused the cause of their fellows during these days.

The antiforeign feelings of the past were not completely forgotten. Within the church itself there was a growing feeling of desire for indigenous control and self-determination. Missionaries with natural conservatism talked much of "devolution" and discussed how rapidly this should be encouraged, but all were accepting the idea of a self-governing, self-supporting, and self-propagating church as the eventual goal. It was no longer a matter of just winning individual converts. There were the corporate concerns of the servants of God in the Body of Christ. The Christian church was established in China with the weakening factors of many competing denominations and the reluctance of missionaries to implement indigenization.

Modern state education had been introduced in the last years of the Ching Dynasty, and the new schools, strengthened by the Chinese graduates of universities in Europe and America, prepared the way for the intellectual flowering known as the Chinese Renaissance, which is associated with real vitality of cultural expression. Significantly it raised the spoken language into literary respectability, and with this reform the possibility of ordinary folk becoming literate was much simplified. New magazines and daily newspapers became formative in the thinking of this period.

Beginning in this period Chinese students took on a significant role in national life. The May Fourth Movement was the beginning of the student movement. This started as a demonstration effective in preventing Chinese delegates from signing the Versailles Treaty, part of the terms of which allowed Japan to claim the German interests in China. Student political activity was to run right through to 1950 and may be seen as a patriotic barometer, sensitive to the needs and aspirations of the Chinese people. The student movement has been called the conscience of China as at first it rallied in support of the Nationalist Party's leadership, and then turned to a more revolutionary role as the Nationalist Kuomintang became increasingly fascist, suppressing free speech and open political discussion.

The student movement is important to our story, for Christian intellectuals were part of it, and it was to be in this context that many believers went into the new China as supporters of the Communist revolution.

What of the peasants during these changing years? As for centuries, they continued to bear the burden of the country. The warlords depended on the land tax for their support, and in provinces where the administration was not stable, the peasants' situation was particularly difficult. Pioneer work was done by missionary institutions in agricultural research. This was particularly an emphasis at the Christian University of Nanking. Others were involved in the promotion of cooperatives and a general rural reform and improvement program. But all such projects met with official rebuff, sometimes subtle and evasive and sometimes more open, as the landlords resisted change. They often controlled the secret societies that in turn had gained a strong grip on the countryside. So Republican China, perforce perhaps, continued to ride on the backs of the peasants.

UNIFICATION AND STRUGGLE 1920-1936

The End of the Journey (written by Mao Tse-tung when the Long March was coming to an end)

The sky is high, the clouds are winnowing,
I gaze southwards at the wild geese disappearing over the horizon.
I count on my fingers, a distance of twenty thousand *li*.
I say we are not heroes if we do not reach the Great Wall.
Standing on the highest peak of Six Mountains,
The red flag streaming in the west wind,
Today with a long rope in my hand,
I wonder how soon before we can bind up the monster.[1]

* * *

There had to be a revolution in China. Why did it prove to be Communist?

Sun Yat-sen and the Nationalist Party or Kuomintang had their base in south China where, as in the north, there was much local division and little real unity. The Chinese industrialists were increasingly looking to Dr. Sun for leadership. But both Britain and the United States dismissed Sun Yat-sen as a crackpot with no capacity to provide leadership for China, and they continued to deal with the northern coterie of militarists who kept jockeying for influence and power.

Dr. Sun, having been rebuffed by Britain and the United States, turned in 1923 to the Soviet Union as the only hope for financial support. The Soviet had just emerged from a successful revolution and was still consolidating the economic base of the new Communist regime, but had made a general statement that it was prepared to treat the Chinese as equals in all respects. Without a surplus of capital funds, Moscow sent some military supplies and some advisors.

During this period there was a group of intellectuals in Peking who were attracted to Marxist thought and the study of the philosophy of Hegel as well as of Western social thought. Into this Chinese metaphysics was blended. Both Chen Tu-hsiu and Li Ta-chao, who were to be the founders of the Chinese Communist Party, were northern intellectuals who, like those they eventually gathered about them, were sons of middle-class or mandarin families, several of landlord origin. In 1915 Professor Li, as an added activity to his teaching of history in a Peking university, started a study group, "The Society for the Study of Marxism." Mao Tsetung, of peasant origin and holding a teachers' college diploma, was then assistant librarian in the university and used all his spare time in an avid pursuit of knowledge. In the study group and the stronger organization to follow, there was much ideological disagreement, as each thinker brought different emphases to bear. Out of this study group grew a party in Peking which is generally regarded as the beginning of the Chinese Communist Party. Independent groups sprang up in Canton, in Shanghai, and in Hunan.

In June, 1920, the first Comintern agent, Gregory Voitinsky, arrived to help with the Party development. He took up residence in Shanghai, where the First Party Congress was held secretly in July, 1921, and the second a year later. After this a definite proposal was made to Sun Yat-sen for collaboration with the Kuomintang, a policy approved by the Comintern.

Dr. Sun proved a hard bargainer and insisted on prior loyalty to the Kuomintang over that to the Chinese Communist Party. Finally it was agreed that members of the Chinese Communist Party *as individuals* could also be members of the Kuomintang, but that they should pledge themselves not to act as a bloc within the Nationalist ranks. This was agreed, but the alliance was at best an uneasy yoking of strongly opinionated partners. At this period, August, 1923, Chiang Kai-shek, as a promising young officer, was sent to study in Moscow by Dr. Sun.[2]

Meanwhile, Sun Yat-sen was endeavoring to come to some agreement with the northern generals, but it was while he was in Peking in 1925 that he died. His legacy to his people was to prove even more influential than his leadership during the early years of the Republic. His book, *The Three Principles of the People,* and his will summoned his compatriots to the completion of his task with the challenge, "The revolution is not completed. Our comrades must strive on." This was to be repeated at every school assembly held in Kuomintang China until its sturdy challenge degenerated to mere ritual.

The Kuomintang was to emerge from these years as the one hope for a unified China, out of the welter of discord that was apparent on all sides. Relations with Japan and Western nations were deteriorating.

Within the Chinese Communist Party there was also division. The weight of numbers and Comintern influence were backing labor-union organization on the assumption that it should be the industrial proletariat that would be the agent of the revolution. Mao Tse-tung was even dropped from the party rolls because of his advocacy of a peasant based revolution. Northern warlords continued their individualist activities, and unity for China seemed far away.

Meanwhile, within the Whampoa Military Academy, a new army leadership was being trained—patriots all, members of the two co-operating parties. Chiang Kai-shek, as the most able of the army officers, became President of the Academy, and to him was given the leadership of the Northern Expedition, which was to march to Peking and bring the northern generals to heel. The Dean of the Academy was Chou En-lai, at present the premier of the People's Republic of China. Chiang set out according to the Kuomintang plan, a plan in the formulation of which the Communist members of this party had shared. Progress to the Yangtze went according to blueprint. Particularly at Nanking foreign property and personnel suffered seriously. Then Chiang received an offer from the industrial and business interests in Shanghai, an offer of their support for a specific concession. He turned eastward to Shanghai, which fell to him with the cooperation of the joint forces, part of which was the Communist underground. In this city Chiang concluded an agreement with the industrialists, the terms of which involved Chiang's pledge that he would expel all Communist elements from the Kuomintang. This agreement made, he did not then proceed north but turned to the task of liquidating the Communists.

Breaking with the Communist elements in the Kuomintang and also with the Soviet advisors at the Whampoa Academy, Chiang set up his capital at Nanking. The new financial support he had gained made it possible to extend his control throughout Central China, and a further shift in international alignment swung the Anglo-American interests behind Chiang as well. His armies continued northward, and a nominal unification of the country was achieved.

In 1929, when the great financial crash came for the West, factories in the treaty ports closed down. Only Japan seemed untouched by the crisis and ready to take advantage both of the international vacuum created and also of Chiang's preoccupation with his effort to run the Communists within China quite literally to the ground. In 1931, Japan moved without hindrance into Manchuria, where she was soon to establish what was virtually to prove a Japanese colonial regime.

By this time Mao Tse-tung was back in the Communist Party, and indeed in 1931 became chairman. Because of his familiarity with the Hunan countryside, he was able to give leadership to the Communist armies in evading the repeated Kuomintang attacks. Chiang's Fifth Annihilation Campaign was conducted with the strategic thoroughness of a scorched earth policy. No tree or dwelling was left standing behind the Kuomintang advance, so there would be no danger of the mobile Communists escaping. This was in 1933. Thus the Long March began. Pursued by the Nationalist divisions, the refugees fled south and, by a circuitous route around the west of Szechuan, up to their eventual destination at Yenan in northern Shensi. This feat of human endurance and suffering remains for Communist history "an emotional mountain peak."[3] Some thirty thousand of the main column traveled six thousand miles, always under threat of pursuit and traversing very difficult terrain. The trail of their progress was marked for years by the memory of the bloodshed and destruction along the route, for both armies had to live off the country as they went.

There were places where the loyalty and co-operation of the peasantry was won by the Communists. This was particularly true in the north, where Mao Tse-tung and the leaders of Chinese communism were to settle for fifteen years of practical experience in working out their doctrines with the people of that region.

It is very important to an understanding of the triumphant Red army and the mode of its conquest to know something of the character of these years when, in effect, the Chinese Communists were isolated from the outside world, including the Soviet Union. Mao's development ideologically came during this period, and it is interesting to note that his authority on guerrilla warfare was a Chinese fighter of the second century B.C.

Robert Payne, in his biography of Mao Tse-tung, comments on the effects of this period of isolation, pointing out that when the Chinese Communist Party eventually became the rulers in Peking, they really did not realize the extent to which even "capitalist" America had moved from unbridled free enterprise to the framework of a welfare state.

Meanwhile the Japanese shadow was falling across the Chinese landscape. A strong group among the Nationalist generals thought that Chiang, instead of exhausting his military resources and the endurance of the people in pursuing the Communist armies, should now turn to the real defense of the nation against the foreign invader. While fighting was going on near the lines of Communist retreat to the north, a young officer, Chang Hsueh-liang, and some others kidnaped Chiang Kai-shek.

A message was despatched to the Communists in Yenan to ask for representatives to attend a court-martial of the prisoner. Accounts vary greatly here, but whatever the motive, be it Mao's awareness that only in Chiang could be found the figure to unify the country, or be it orders from Stalin that Chiang was to be spared, or the softening of heart because of the courageous intercession of Madame Chiang, or simply that Chiang agreed to the terms, the incident ended with Chiang Kai-shek again in control and committed to resistance against Japan. On Christmas Day, 1936, he walked out of the city with the pledge of a unified country behind him, ready to defend China against Japanese aggression.

UNITED FRONT, 1936-1946

1936 Robin Hood

A young bandit and his men had systematically robbed the rich. The takings had been distributed to the poor. Before this eighteen-year-old youth was shot in the public square, he stated to those watching, "As long as the poor people suffer, and as long as there is oppression, extortion, and corruption in the countryside, this sort of thing will go on!"

* * *

This was a moving period in China, Nationalist China. The Yenan (Communist) armies were to become the Eighth Route Army under the one generalissimo, and it was true that Chiang Kai-shek and Madame Chiang Kai-shek became figures symbolic of a China with a new determination and a new hope. They were taken to the hearts of the people and were the inspiration of the New Life Movement, with its disciplines of self-denial and simple living to strengthen the national cause. The Generalissimo became the President of the Republic, under the Kuomintang Party administration.

The fact that Chiang Kai-shek had become a baptized Christian when he joined the Methodist Church of his wife's family was a source of great encouragement to the various branches of the church in China and also a significant factor in attitudes of Western people toward him. He and his wife became international hero figures, an image reflected strongly in missionary literature.

In 1937 the Japanese pushed from the north down to Shanghai. The Sino-Japanese War had begun. Chiang was forced to move his government toward the western mountains, finally digging into the rocky hill of Chungking city in western China. Resistance morale was still high, as demonstrated by the trek of university students and professors with what of their precious libraries and equipment they could carry from coastal campuses. There was a determined effort to keep education going against the day of peace when China would need her leaders. There was much of heroism, of enthusiasm, and of self-sacrifice for high causes.

And still the Japanese pressed on, still the Japanese bombers brought terror from the Chinese sky. The Christian church joined in the resistance program, and in the West rallied to the refugee situation, particularly for educational institutions. Student relief was administered through the student divisions of the Y.M.C.A. and the Y.W.C.A., and secretaries were appointed to carry on group activities with Christian students and for the many who were inquirers. Probably there were more open doors to the gospel then than at any other time in Chinese history. It was during the war years that student Christian fellowships grew up in many of the national universities, some of which continued their witness long into the People's Republic.

Friendly feelings for the Western nations were strengthened when Japan attacked Pearl Harbor, bringing China into the allied cause of World War II. As American armed might became effective, China was given much greater assistance. Where villages were near the front lines of the Chinese Eighth Army, the people were often drawn into the guerrilla activities, but generally they simply suffered the hated alien military rule and carried on as best they could.

Stories were told of Christian groups coming together across denominational lines for a stronger fellowship in this situation. The missionary personnel had withdrawn with the advance of the enemy, but the Chinese church itself remained, meeting the needs of its own people for fellowship and worship. After the war the denominational missionaries returned, and this wartime fellowship and corporate experience often broke down as each believer was drawn back to his own particular fold.

The move to the West, to Free China, bound Chiang Kai-shek and his Kuomintang officials even more closely to the landlord and capitalist classes. The war expenditures were a drain that only tightened the belts of the ordinary man. Against this the black market and wartime corruption made many wealthy over night. Printing more money was the easiest way to meet government bills, and inflation flared. Attempts at devaluation and a new standard of currency just started the process all over again.

Politically the group known as the Chen clique came into the ascendancy. The Chens were strongly reactionary and brought increasingly powerful pressures to bear upon all educational institutions. For instance, the book *China's Destiny* was published under Chiang Kai-shek's name in 1943. An English edition was quickly withdrawn when reviewers pointed out alarming fascist tendencies, and it was ruled that foreign correspondents could not even cable parts of it abroad. But every Chinese high school and university student in the Kuomintang areas had to pass examinations on it, either to get into or to graduate from school. Throughout the school system firm controls for politically doctrinaire views became more and more evident. A regulation, not always enforced, required that school principals should be members of the Kuomintang Party.

The privations of ordinary student rations together with the difficulty of getting textbooks and adequate materials for laboratories and for library reference meant that the whole, heroically retained university system unavoidably lowered its standards. Yet it was in the universities and through the student movement that the conscience of the people spoke. It was here that prophetic voices were heard, raising a protest at the increasingly fascist pressures in Free China. Their reward was repression.

Secret police raids were made by night. Professors disappeared from their homes and students from their dormitories.[4] Thought control and political orthodoxy of the narrowest and most cramping sort were enforced on the whole educational system through class teachers who were responsible for reading the weekly diaries of students and for trying to ferret out all disloyal thoughts. This was the time of the "White Terror."

After Pearl Harbor the Kuomintang reasoning seemed to be "Why bother about Japan? America is going to look after this enemy, anyway. We'll wait for our own civil war, and get ready." Arms and supplies were stored for future use, and a special group of army cadets was trained, not in modes of fighting suitable against the Japanese but in other ways pointing to domestic conflict. Was it any wonder then that a depressing pall of despair seemed to settle over the youth of the land? If they responded to the needs of their country, they were rebuffed, and often on graduation their hard-won qualifications did not seem to be wanted.

And in the north the Eighth Route Army under Mao Tse-tung kept on fighting the Japanese. Chungking sent no supplies, but the ingenuity and resourcefulness of the years since the Long March had left the Communists sturdier, more disciplined, and more inventive. Guerrilla warfare was easy for them to develop. They had worked with the peasant and helped him reclaim land. They had shared with him their entertainment and their ideas. They were developing the practical expression of their ideology in a small compass of rural administration. They fought the Japanese with Japanese weapons, and they maintained their fighting trim and morale. The soldiers not only fought, but they studied and knew why they fought. Was it any wonder that many students glanced northward?

Whatever one feels about Communist theory, the fact was that by 1945 when V-J Day came, Mao Tse-tung, Chu-Teh, and the old-line Communists with their fighting army were fit and strong, ready for what lay ahead.

REVOLUTION, 1947-1949

Acedia

1949: SEPTEMBER IN CHUNGKING

". . . We knew inside our bellies why nothing was painted, nothing worked. There was no need to talk. Chungking was waiting, waiting to be liberated, or waiting to fall, depending which of the two equally meaningless words one chose to use. It had given up before it was taken. It was waiting in turpitude, in sloth, in corruption. The place had lost heart. Acedia, the sin of the soul, the spiritual torpor . . . was infecting not one man but a whole city. The people had lost faith in the faithless government that was now announcing its last stand, a fight to the finish, but whose efforts other than vocal were entirely concerned with preparations for flight to safety."[5]

* * *

V-J Day brought peace to the Asian theater of World War II, but for China the cessation of world-wide hostilities meant the reopening of the civil struggle. So it was that when the conversations and negotiations, the international pressures and diplomacy failed to bring a coalition settlement, the Kuomintang and the Red armies were fighting each other.

The Communist armies spread over the whole area with surprising speed, so swiftly in fact that their administrative procedures and personnel were sorely taxed to set up the machinery of government as they advanced. Chiang and his supporters quit the country by plane to Taiwan taking with them those who could afford such flight.

Missionaries had to decide whether to remain into the new regime or to leave before the Communists arrived. Many of these ex-China folk moved to Taiwan to carry on their work among Chinese-speaking peoples there.

A further factor which strengthens the tendency to a polarization between the Christians of Taiwan and those of People's China is the fact that very naturally it has been those most critical of communism who have streamed to Taiwan, so that Christians with the theological basis which sees in communism the anti-Christ, the beast of Revelation, are drawn to Taiwan.

Some of us continued in People's China, feeling that God would use his servants there too. We came to feel that on leaving the mainland we could not go to Taiwan to continue work, because of the political interpretation which would be given to this action in China itself and which would make it all the more difficult for the Christian church in People's China to carry on.

Here too we knew we had to respect the integrity of our missionary colleagues who did decide it was right to carry on their work in Taiwan.

One further word before we turn to a discussion of the new China. "Colonialism" and "imperialism" are words of bitterness in Communist China for Christians as well as ordinary Chinese, but they are words with strong emotional content in all of Asia and increasingly in Africa too. The white man has been responsible for colonialism and the trappings of obvious imperialism. He now must bear the brunt of the rejection of the system with which he has been identified.

And the reaction is often expressed in unreasonable and exaggerated terms. For instance, the Asian-African Conference at Bandung in 1954 embodied the new orientation, and it is instructive for us of the West to take such events and the statements made by such conferences very soberly and with understanding.

These ideas are expressed in an open letter to all Christians in North America, from a group of Chinese Christians in Kuomintang China, a letter brought to America by a Chinese Christian and reprinted by a group of American Christians at private expense.

Shanghai, April 4, 1948

DEAR FELLOW-CHRISTIANS OF AMERICA,

Time is running short and the decisive moment for the Chinese church is imminent. We, a group of leading Christians in China, being clergymen and laymen of five denominations, feel impelled to speak to you, not as representatives of official bodies but as individual Christians, concerning our unspeakable anxiety as regards the future of our church in China and as regards the part you can play to make things easier for us. . . .

. . . While we have complete confidence in the unchanged good will of the millions of you kind-hearted American Christians, the changes in the Chinese people's sympathies and aspirations have been so drastic that old patterns of thinking are no longer workable and can indeed do great harm to the cause of spreading the gospel among our people. . . . Are we not to be held responsible if we allow our generosity and good will to be exploited and turned into nothing but an investment in hatred? Should we not now so beware that the message of God's salvation is presented in such a way that we do not unnecessarily give the non-Christian world a reason to label the Church once again as a weapon of power politics. . . ?

We feel sorry to say that more and more we have been led by hard facts to the conviction that there are in the American church certain leaders with definite political ambitions whose activities in the name of the Church on behalf of interests other than religious are not only detrimental to the traditional good friendship the Chinese have for America, but also take away from our preaching its convincing power and make the gospel a laughing stock to our youth. The entire future of our Church in China is too sacred to be made into a gamble. Thus, we can hardly afford not to plead to you and, through you, to your Mission Boards and church authorities for co-operation and understanding. We sincerely hope you will be sympathetic with us in our present difficulties and embarrassment, as we are the ones who have to go into direct contact with the common people of China at the outposts of the Christian frontiers. The common people of China today are not slumbering and should not be treated as such. They have a right to ask whether we preach the gospel out of the eternal love of God for men which transcends national and partisan interests, and not out of some lower and negative political calculation, or whether there is some political design mixed up in our evangelistic mission.

First, we assert that there is no Church issue at stake or in any way involved in the present conflict itself, unless we ourselves choose to gear the fate of the Church to that of a particular politico-military group. American Christians can help relieve our embarrassment if your Mission Boards can be urged to declare that they disassociate themselves from the China policy of their government. This will strengthen us greatly in China in our witnessing for the gospel.

Second, we ask for a more vigorous application of Christian restraint in making judgments when facts are not sufficiently reliable. While we must not for one moment neglect the prophetic mission of the Church in the world let us remind ourselves that we have to be fair, precise, detached and motivated by good will. . . .

Third, we request you to pray for us daily so that the Chinese Church may possess the courage of its conviction and may witness for Christ against unrighteousness anywhere. . . . We are going through a most trying period of our history and your prayers are much needed.

Fourth, if there is any group in China today for which Christian prayers have been the most denied, it is the Chinese communists, our "enemy," our fellow-countrymen and our fellow-children of God in spite of the fact that they have refused to believe in Him as we do.

We have much for which to repent before God for what we have done and for what we have left undone which have contributed to make the situation as it is. Aside from other matters may God open our eyes to see much of their constructive work for our people in North China which should humble us. While we pray for God's forgiveness of our lack of good will and prejudice, let us also beg Him to pour down His Spirit to complete what is amiss, and to correct all that is not of God but of men's own self-righteousness. . . .

We wish that there may be a mighty tide of prayers across America for the mentioned purposes. It is obviously unwise for us to sign our names to this open letter. But, please do not let this be made into a reason not to take our requests seriously. It is most unfortunate that freedom of expression has been curtailed to such an extent that even we, in Christian love, cannot but withhold our identity. We assure you that we in this letter do represent the aspirations and opinions of very many alert Christians in China today and hope that, before very long, there will be a way to make known who are the writers.

Yours in Christ,
Fifteen Chinese Christians,
including clergymen of three denominations, professors of sociology, welfare leaders, businessmen, and high school principals.

5 · *The "New" China*

BEGINNINGS, 1951

Thousands of the female rural militia came to the city to celebrate. Many of these little farm women had never before been out of their hamlets and openly enjoyed the marvels of the city with the delightful naïveté of the country bumpkin. The schools of the city provided accommodation, and there was a great welcome for the marching women. There were displays and the spring fair to attend as well as the official parades. A special exhibit of pre- and post-natal child development and care was prepared by the university department in child care. Each little country woman was taken through this exhibit and, with the aid of lecture and individual explanation, was given a complete and very frank course in sex education and child development. A display of drugs helped the uninitiated to distinguish the reliable from the inferior production. From these women there was jubilant appreciation, "We never had a government that cared for us before!"

* * *

A woman professor had attended an assembly of the Women's Federation, a semiofficial body, pledged to the welfare of women and children. She came back much impressed. The professor went on to say, "What a shame that you foreigners are not welcome in so many places and can see none of the good things that are going on!" Later she sighed and said, "We who have studied abroad may never really be trusted by this regime, but it is better for the common people, and we must give it our support and loyalty and the service of all our skills."

* * *

We now come to the events that brought the Chinese Communists to power, the "Liberation," as it is referred to both by Chinese Communists and ordinary folk. For many it was in truth a freeing. We may feel that the term is hypocritical and false because a Communist regime seems of necessity to deny so much that is precious to us, but our own historical alternatives have little in common with the actual choices before the Chinese people in 1949 and 1950. For the majority the liberation promise was a vast improvement. For a significant minority it was to be much worse.

Mao Tse-tung proclaimed the establishment of the "People's Republic of China" on October 1, 1949, and by the end of that year he visited Moscow, the first time this leader had stepped outside his native China. By June the Korean War had started.

Thus China was "liberated" by the People's army. There was not much fighting during these months, though here and there the Nationalist armies returned the fire for a brief period. But there was plenty of violence and slaughter on both sides. As the Nationalists withdrew, their political prisoners were killed rather than taken along. In some cases the bodies found showed evidences of torture and brutal treatment. These reminders of the "White Terror" in years of strict Kuomintang political repression did not soften the vindictiveness of the triumphant forces. The latter were, however, better disciplined than any troops in China's history, and "justice" was to be meted out in the emotional orgy of the mass trial or later in the people's courts, when the crimes of the antirevolutionaries were sifted according to firm, if ruthless, procedure.

We in Chengtu were "liberated" on Christmas Day, 1949. It had been a time of anxiety, uncertainty, and general demoralization. There was a strange relief that the past months were behind, with the hopelessness and enervation that came as the Kuomintang lost its capacity to inspire its people to carry on even the ordinary tasks of everyday life.

Slowly Chengtu adjusted to the new rule. The soldiers who had come in were sturdy northerners, disciplined, and—as generally throughout the country—they paid their way. The zealous attacked the custom of rickshaw riding, the only mode of public transportation then existing, but which to them was a denial of human brotherhood and dignity. Riders were forced to take turns pulling the erstwhile coolie, a measure that soon made the populace fearful of riding, and rickshaw pullers faced serious unemployment. Finally high-ranking officers riding in rickshaws tried to reassure the people.

There were public statements about the wrongs of rickshaw transportation. But there was also a recognition that this was a heritage of the old society, which would eventually be replaced by a public bus system. Until that time and until there was the development of industries for the fuller employment of the rickshaw puller, it was a patriotic act to use the rickshaw in the city. This illustrates the interaction of reform idealism with the flexibility often shown by the Chinese Communist regime, realistically sensitive to how much change can be accepted at once.

At first the city was heavily guarded with a network of soldiers and police on practically very corner. An early regulation "froze" both property and persons. In other words, you could not move baggage or furniture or change your residence, or even sleep at a friend's for the night, without reporting to the police. This strait jacket did have its function in bringing order to society and prevented the monied or landlord classes from a further scattering of their possessions. Gradually a process of information and education took place as street groups were drawn together and local cadres joined in endless and patient discussion.

Some months later there was no further need for police patrols. Discipline was transferred to the populace, and as the street groups gained a corporate sense there were many grassroots projects, such as the repaving activity when labor was freely contributed by the street residents. There was conscious and spontaneous co-operation between citizen and administration, with a good deal of pride in achievement. One day while walking along a fresh bit of sidewalk, I found a string blocking the way. An old lady, spinning in her doorway, called out, "That's *our* street. It's drying. You can't walk on it." So people gradually claimed the life of the city as their own, and eventually in the country a new sense of confidence was born.

Perhaps of more significance were some of the general ways in which the new administration won the active co-operation of the people. On the national level there was the fact of peace and unification under a stable government, things which the Chinese people had not enjoyed since the days of the Empire. Then economic life was stabilized with some astute and effective measures, introduced slowly so that the implementation strengthened the faith of the ordinary man in the government's banks, and with just the necessary regulation and threat of force to bring results.

Early in the regime Chengtu citizens joined in subscribing to Victory Bonds, and enthusiastic patriots competed to see who could sell the most. One needs to remember that the Chinese suspected that the Communist regime had come to stay, and the quality that Mao Tse-tung was to analyze in his short essay "On Practice" is an essential Chinese pragmatism: the ability to adjust realistically to the inevitable. Chinese philosophy idealizes the bamboo, which bends in a storm but doesn't break. Compromise is the effective way to meet a challenge. The Victory Bond collection for our school was headed by the teacher who was in charge of Christian activities for the girls, and she was esteemed at this time because of her record in collecting subscriptions for reconstruction.

Meantime, there was an interesting saving offer that acted like a magnet to the bits of money tucked away in jars and secret corners. Under this plan the value of your savings was tied to the cost of living index. If the cost of living index rose so did your capital sum, and if it was steady you got the interest. If it decreased your capital divided into a credit of more units. One could not lose. This banking offer was significant both in its restoration of confidence in the banks and the government, and also in the effectiveness through which it drew the savings from secret corners into public finance.

Early in the regime the landed classes were required to refund the deposit fees that tenants had to pay landlords as security. This measure had significant results. For the provident landowner with ready cash, there was no difficulty, although he had to turn over large sums to the Farmer's Association, a nongovernment but official body for the administration of land reform. The money to be returned on the deposit accounts did not go back directly to the farmer but was held for him by the Farmer's Association. Funds were then available for specified productive purposes—a new water buffalo, a much needed plow, or some other tool, but not for an expedition to town or a spending spree.

Landlords who had no ready money were pressed into selling possessions. In our city at this time, it was common to see stalls outside wealthy homes with luxury garments, costly furniture, Parker pens, Rolex watches, diamonds and other jewels, all on sale for whatever the bidder would offer. Since the monied groups were under pressure and certainly not adding to their possessions, and since speculators realized the inadvisability of stocking up on luxury goods, the only people who could buy were the working class and the poor. Our servants, who had never before had more than cotton padded garments for winter chill, now invested in warm fur-lined gowns of excellent quality.

This measure then, without direct government regulation or control, resulted in an almost immediate redistribution of the good things of the land.

CONSOLIDATION

The People's Republic of China is now in its second decade. Many visitors and observers have regarded the revolution of 1949 as the most significant event in the long history of the Chinese nation, and some feel that the impact of the Communist ideology will destroy the rich culture of one of the world's oldest civilizations.[1] Discontinuity and change are part of the New China. However, as the years have rolled on and the Peking government's policy and aspirations have developed, continuities may also be noted—some subtle, some bold, as the Peking government intentionally reclaims the past glories of an almost Asia-wide hegemony.

A total perspective on this vast country must take in the flow of her history as well as the immediate developments of the twentieth century. Even in the early, uncertain years of the People's Republic, one observed a cycle of disturbance and then—perhaps with a new focus—a settlement back into old patterns. This was true of the schools. Chinese education has always been directed to conformity. The stream of continuity remains strong. Recent books that attempt to appraise the character and strength of the new China are tending to recognize more and more of the continuities.[2] One often wondered which of two great forces would be stronger in its continuing impact on the developments in China in our time, the powerful force of the new ideas unleashed with the coming of the Communist revolution, or the basic personality pattern of the Chinese people. China for centuries has conquered her conquerors. Will this be true of a new ideological conquest as it was of dynastic rulers in the past? Let us turn to several aspects of contemporary China for illustration.

Propaganda or Education?

The educational by-product of any regulation is never forgotten in People's China. Always we were aware of a concern to involve the people of the country consciously and with informed knowledge in the affairs of the land. Every measure was patiently interpreted. No Chinese any longer has the freedom to be ignorant, silent, or detached.

A good illustration of this educational process may be seen in the country-wide attack on cholera. We learned from all the mass communications media—the newspapers, street bulletins, radio outlets on the streets, and organized study groups—that everyone was to get inoculated. This was necessary we were told to preserve the health of the nation. Individuals had to think of their responsibility toward others as well as for keeping their own health. A time limit was announced during which one could secure inoculations from hospitals or doctors as one wished. Then medical teams set up simultaneous roadblocks on all the main arteries of the city, and everyone had to produce his certificate of inoculation or get his needle right there on the street. Not only was the inoculation given, but also a little lecture on the need of this protection and the nature of the disease symptoms and treatment. Then the person involved was expected to answer questions on the lesson before being allowed to go on his way.

There were, of course, arrests in this period, for in our part of the territory there were many remnants of the Kuomintang administration. But the fearfulness of the common people gradually changed to reassurance and confidence. The new ideology was introduced through the basic text, *Development of Society*. This gave the Marxist analysis of social history in broad, sweeping terms and very simply. The common man began to feel himself very much a part of a great country, with a new sense of his own class, if not of his own individual importance.

Everything in People's China, then, is conscientiously explained, rationalized, and driven home. From the first days of this government, there have been varied emphases, and in each case they have been carried into every political study group, so that every citizen knows not only that such and such a law has been passed, but what it deals with and, more fundamentally, why it is important. In land reform too everyone was made aware of why this economic program was necessary, all the blessings it would bring, and that it was the Communist Party under Mao Tse-tung that made it all possible.

The men in the Peking government are very astute in using a situation to strengthen their cause, and manage to "play by ear" to the country's response very faithfully. The people are called upon to kill flies because the American enemy had sent them into China. The people responded. This psychological motivation and satisfaction were very effective for carrying on an urgent public health campaign. Here was an emotional drive that would carry out the program with utter thoroughness.

One reason why I have felt we could probably accept the People's Government's own figures on political executions and liquidations is that, here again, these were part of ideological and patriotic training. The antirevolutionaries were gathered up in a vast net on the night of March 25, 1951. Then gradually the sifting took place as each was examined and guilt assessed. For the political criminal the legal process did not involve the appearance of the accused for his own defense; one was really guilty until proved innocent. Or perhaps it would be fairer to the Chinese interpretation to say that one would not be arrested if not guilty.

Then in the summer of 1951, there was a progressive amnesty proclaimed. Those sentenced to death because of complicity in the death of a Communist had their penalty commuted for a period of two years, during which thought reform or heavy labor would be their lot, with a reappraisal at the end of the period. Hard labor is regarded not merely as punishment but also purging. One can thus become a new person and ready for new ideas. The political criminals with lesser guilt had a comparable scaling down of their penalties, but in each case the changed loyalty seemed to be the focus of attention. A self-confident country has no need to cloak its violence, when violence can be turned to educational purpose.

In this context of ideological remolding, we are reminded of emphases in the development of the People's regime during its first decade, for political, economic, and international developments are all reflected in the study program and propaganda of the day. The Three-Anti Movement against corruption, waste, and bureaucratism, which particularly applied to party members as numbers increased rapidly in the early fifties, was followed by the land reform laws and the Five-Anti Movement of 1952, a drive against bribery, tax evasion, stealing state property, theft of economic secrets, and embezzlement in carrying out government contracts. This emphasis resulted in the liquidation of many business firms and the placing of industrial enterprises more firmly under government control.

The socialization tendencies in agriculture were paralleled in similar directions in the urban and industrial scene under the five-year plans, the first running from 1953-1957, and the second beginning in 1957 with a blueprint for production up to 1962. Generally the goals of the first plan were exceeded. But reports suggest that the goals of the second were set too high in spite of the herculean effort of the Great Leap Forward, which took place in 1958, when communes and even universities were encouraged to develop small factories and blast furnaces. Visitors to China at that time speak of the impression of a whole nation putting forth tremendous effort. "Twenty years in a day" was another phrase of this period. "Walking on two feet" refers to the policy to develop heavy industry and an agricultural economy at the same time.

It is apparent that the class which continues to bear the weight of China's development is, as of old, the peasant, and this will remain true until greater attention can be given to light industry with the goal of turning out consumer products. So far the loyalty of the peasant has been sufficiently pledged to Mao Tse-tung to carry the program, though what the strain of many years of further privation and famine may do remains to be seen. Continuing foreign threat provides plenty of excuse for privation as the needs for defense necessitate heavy industrial development, and international competition means a priority given for a sizeable expenditure on atomic research.

All these emphases may be seen not merely as pointing to a strong and ruthless totalitarian regime determined to get its own way, but as part of a new paternalism that knows what is really good for people and plans for them in terms of this responsibility. There are dreams and clearly articulated goals, which perhaps are new to China. But the paternalism is a familiar feature, quite continuous with the past. It is interesting to follow the thought of one writer who suggests that the ancient philosophy of Yang-Yin, the balance of the opposites, of light and dark, of male and female, of good and evil, falls into an indigenous concept of a dialectic interaction with the *Tao* or the Way, conceived as the eventual mode for society, changing with each of these interactions.[3] Through the brief years of the Communist regime in China, there is a definite dialectical relation between the policies of the government and the awareness of the masses, between the economic development of the country and the advisability of pushing on to the next stage, between the international climate and China's own response or withdrawal.

Internally the programs of physical reconstruction and development have contributed to the confidence of the populace in their government. We read of projects for flood control, for irrigation and reforestation, and the building of many miles of roads and railways. This means that the distribution of food particularly can be more equitable. Of old there were occasions when there was plenty of food in one part of the country but no possibility of getting it where needed, because the carrier would eat up his load before getting it to the destination. Today the government can make substantial claims for the overseeing of distribution and for the implementation of an effective rationing system, though some reports indicate drastic shortages.

The fact that the worker's blue boiler suit is inexpensive is probably the consideration which makes it universal, more than the effort to stamp out all variety in clothing. The mass-patterned garment is cheap to purchase, and personal money can be saved for other things.

Mention should be made of the policy of relaxation which marked the period known from the phrase, "Let flowers of many kinds blossom, diverse schools of thought contend." This became the theme of the policy speech delivered on May 26, 1958, by Lu Tin-yi of the Propaganda Department of the Central Committee of the Communist Party. This speech advocated freedom for independent thinking and debate, especially in the realms of art, literature, and science.

The result of this pronouncement was a loosing, of the intellectuals particularly, in a flood of free speech and criticism. Some analysts regard this announcement as a clear device to locate the laggards in political loyalty and see it as a successful trap for the unwary who really took the government at its word and spoke out. Others, however, feel that the party leadership was not aware of the actual extent of resistance, and that they were considerably taken aback at the flood of criticisms that flowed in, some even directed at the Communist Party policy and leadership itself. A firm check was given and the free flowering period came to an abrupt end.

It is not hard to see how this train of events would involve the Christians in China; first the relaxation, with its implications for freer speech, and then the tight rein, which sieved out another group of persons to be classified as disloyal. And the pattern of conformity was strengthened again.

What place has freedom of speech in a conformist society? The announcement of the "hundred flowers," as it came to be known, suggested that there was a real contribution in freely proffered criticism that would arrest mistakes. Freedom and denial of freedom are difficult to define, as so much depends upon the acceptance of the bounds beyond which one cannot go—what in any state may be called "sedition."

An incident on a river boat brought the nature of freedom of speech home to some of us. There were two young women aboard, each wearing the worker's garb and each with two children, bound for the northeast where they were to join their husbands who were already working on a government assignment. One night a motley collection of deck passengers, about two hundred of us, were lying awake as the small steamer had moored for the night. In the lull before we dropped off to sleep, one of the women said, "You know, the way we are carrying out the land reform is not good. In my part of the country, it is terrible the things they do to the landlords and their wives!" I thought that the sky would fall or that the speaker would be annihilated by some mass action or protest. But there was quiet, and she went on to describe inhumanities and tortures. Finally the second woman spoke with reproof, "Don't be silly. The landlords have been the oppressors of the peasants for hundreds of years. They are the targets of the revolution and deserve everything they get." And the two women talked back and forth for a while, with the first speaker crowning her argument against the bitter treatment with the convincing assurance, "Besides, Mao Tsetung wouldn't like it!" Her view of the benevolent father of his people was clear.

The conversation ended when a young liberation army soldier asked the second speaker, "Are you by any chance of a landlord family yourself?" "Yes, both myself and my husband are landlords' children, but we have been 'progressive' and have given everything to the country." And so the ex-landlord's daughter could only carefully espouse the official line, or what she felt was the correct thing to say. The woman of the people was actually free to say what she thought, because her loyalty had never been in question. So it is that many Chinese, wistful for some of the ease of the old days for themselves, will say, "The next generation will be fine. They will always have known the present, and for them it will be natural and accepted, and they will feel quite free!"

Thought Reform

"Brain washing" is a term with frightening connotations for us. In China reaction to this phrase is not so negative, for the Chinese words themselves suggest a washing that is a purgative cleansing of old evil, rather than one that is necessarily violent and accompanied by painful pressures. The notions of reorientation, re-education, and thought reform are less colored words for us and do express what is in many Chinese minds. Probably too there is less use of fear and force than we assume, but there are tremendous social pressures to conform and go along with the people in the glorious new day for the Chinese nation.

The process is one of unwearied discussion, persuasion, and repetition of slogans, as it is carried on at all levels of

Chinese society, in small study and discussion groups, in institutions for re-education, in revolutionary universities, or among the reactionaries in a prison setting. Minds are really channeled into new grooves. In the early days a phrase was in current use which suggested that one could not yet see the light, "his brain has not yet been bored through." The "seeing of the light" for the pseudo-religious functioning of the Communist ideology is almost parallel to the conversion experience of the Christian. Once one accepts the new framework, all else falls into place.

This is not written to minimize the evils of pressures that lead to totalitarian conformity or ideological pressures which are deeply offensive to our tradition of individual liberty and freedom of speech and spirit, but rather to recognize the real impact of this concept in China today. A government does not beat people into line by physical threat alone when it has available the processes which establish inner response and understanding co-operation.[4]

What of the Christian church and its adjustment to the new regime? Let us try to understand as we "listen" to the words of a Chinese who in the years before the Communists came to power had won a deserved reputation as a loyal servant of God.

* * *

The following is the statement of a Chinese Christian educator. Date: 1952 or earlier.

I used to fear that socialism would suppress individual personality and incentive. I have observed among our students how youth has changed since our country started on the road to socialism. I have seen individuals grow in the desire to serve society, each one feeling his or her own part in the changing social order. We intellectuals, who used to stand aloof and advise, now feel deeply moved to join actively in working for the future.

We are not stifled. On the contrary, we are inspired. I am more practical than philosophical. I dislike writing about *why* things should be done; I like doing them. The slogan of the Communist Party for the new regime is: "Serve the people . . ." I like that. To serve people is part of the Christian religion. Formerly I fooled myself that I was serving the people. I certainly wanted to, but it was then just an ideal.

We certainly did little for our ideals. We see now that unless the whole structure is changed, the kind of service we wanted to give could not be done. In the past the church endeavored to give help to the people; it did not enable the people to help themselves. How could that be under landlordism and other oppressions in the old society? It must be admitted that Marxist-Leninist principles help people to help themselves.

I was also moved by a remark by Chairman Mao: "You must first care for the people's private income." It is plain as common sense that when you have cared for the people's private welfare you can get public funds. This explains the basis of the Communists' influence. They seek to ensure the long-range welfare of the people and plan for greater and lasting prosperity. Our revolution is thoroughgoing. It has brought fundamental and total change. The fundamental economic basis of our nation is changed. The philosophy underlying this change is Communist. I believe the government is doing an honest job in helping the people to work for themselves.

I have told you how slow I was to side with the revolution. Two problems blocked my way to working happily with the new regime. One was how to reconcile my Christian religion with Communism and its teachings. The other was my dislike of the mass movement and mass accusation technique. . . . I set out to discover for myself how the missionary movement had been used by imperialist interests in China. We in the church had always felt there was no political purpose in it, but now I see that, consciously or unconsciously, missionaries served imperialism. Archbishop Temple's "Studies in St. John's Gospel" helped me to understand this. I cannot quote the specific passages to you now. At one point he referred to a minister who said that mission work helps the unification of the British Empire. That opened my eyes a bit, but I was fully awakened by Warren Austin's statement at a meeting in the United Nations Assembly. He revealed that one purpose of American religious work in China was to persuade the Chinese people to accept American imperialism. The attitude of Western missionaries towards the war in Korea further enlightened us.

As to the relation of Christian faith and Communist teachings and practice, I have accepted the viewpoint of Dr. Y. T. Wu and the Reform Movement. I have come to see that the aims of Christians and Communists are similar in the practical matters of serving human society. It seems to me we must realize that the Communists have been leaders in this field and that they begin by solving the economic problems fundamentally. They believe that man is capable of changing his environment and reforming the world. Christians depend on God, but much depends on what content you put into the word, "God." Christians also say man must do God's work on earth. Christians say there is a moral purpose in the universe. I no longer have any conflict between this belief and Communist teaching.

* * *

The following is a report from the Enlarged Conference of the National Committee of the Y.W.C.A. of China in March 1950, in Shanghai.[5]

When the Chinese revolution had obtained its victory, when her population had stood up as the master, the National Committee of YWCA facing this situation, held a meeting, which began on March 1, 1950, lasted for ten days. Representatives included volunteers and secretaries from city YWCA's and student YWCA's, total number was about forty, including the Executive Committee members of the National YWCA. We, after having evaluated the past and looking toward the future made sure about our directions hereafter and settled the YWCA direction for the future. From now on the YWCA must follow the peoples' victory and march towards the new historical era.

In the first place, we altogether support the "Common Program and Organic Law" and taking them as our political direction and the people together, fight against the imperialism, feudalism and bureaucratic capitalism, and struggle for her independence, democracy, peace and prosperity. At the same time we, the YWCA have the characteristics of Christianity, and also the "Common Program and Organic Law" say that a people should have the right of thoughts, lecturing, publishing, holding meetings, or organizing a meeting, and religious belief. Now we have all of these and we must respect them and use them to serve the people and against the activities taking the form of religion, but working against the people. . . .

Internationally we must take the policy, which aids to protect the independence, freedom and territory of China; which supports world peace forever, international co-operation, fighting against aggression and war, as the direction of our conduct. . . .

Since the organization of the Chinese Democratic Women's Federation, the Chinese women's movement has united direction and leadership. The YWCA is one member of the federation. So we must now follow their leadership to fulfill our work; to strengthen our organization; to rebuild our thoughts. Let us always think of the people. We should not get away from the people. The YWCA belongs to the people. From this year our work is to follow this direction. In 1950 we want our program to emphasize work in cultural education, productive education. We want to develop a political consciousness, then we will be able to stick together and work for the people.

Dear friends, today is the age of the people. There is only one way to go so we must have the spirit of Christ and follow Chairman Mao under the leadership of the People's Government, and work completely for the establishment of a new Democracy in China.

LAND REFORM

Let us turn to a brief discussion of land reform, which affected the life of the church as it did that of the whole nation. We have traced the preparatory stage when the landlords were required to refund the deposit money of the peasant farmer and the resulting redistribution of material goods. The deposit or security fee received by the landlord over decades, even back as far as the dynastic era, had been paid in various currencies. The new regime settled the rates for repayment in each period, very much to the tenant's or peasant's advantage. If one was an absentee landlord, the requirement was pressed as rigidly as for those on the scene, and this is one of the factors behind the extortion letters we hear of. It is pathetically satiric to note the numbers of Chinese in North America, many of them laundrymen and certainly not in the wealthy group who, with meager savings, purchased land in their own country hoping someday to return. It gave them great psychological security to possess a few acres of land. Now, with the new regime, they had suddenly become absentee landlords against whose accounts large sums were due. Relatives were held accountable in China, so the toll of extortion, suffering, and misunderstanding mounted.

Land reform itself started in the north and was carried on across the country as teams could be prepared and organization set up to handle it. Nearly every intellectual in the country spent his stint at one or two rounds of the reform, and for many this was a deeply formative experience. They gained a sense of the hereditary suffering of the peasant, which came to many as a deep cultural shock. The fact of the upper and middle classes' own involvement in the exploitation of the Chinese peasant was brought home to them. Tireless discussion at every stage meant that most who participated in land reform came out of the experience as different people. Some of our Christian friends came back from land reform, inspired as from a religious revival, and with a very much deepened dedication to serve their own people. Others were quieter about the experience, but it was not hard to guess their relief to have this experience behind.

The teams were composed of a core of the experienced staff or cadres who knew all about the process. Others were assigned by the government for one or more periods. Sometimes former Kuomintang Party members were tested in such an appointment before being given a permanant post. High schools and colleges supported their teachers and professors as they each took three months off for this contribution to the country. In the fall of 1951 the whole staff and student body of the Theological College in Chengtu took their turn.

After a substantial period of orientation in theory and method, each member of the team lived in a farmer's house and shared completely in the life of the peasant. The first task was to break down the farmers' reluctance to accuse the landlords, a disinclination arising in part from fear of reprisal. So confidence had to be given and the activity called *tou tsen* (struggle) was initiated. This was the *su ku* (speak bitterness) period, when the idea was to get out all the old resentments and bitterness of the past. Of course, this meant arousing many memories of injustices done, and the human fact of vindictiveness and profit could not be avoided, though with a certain check because land reform was essentially a group process.

The team members met with their little groups for a week of meetings. One farmer in the group finally spoke his bitterness, then another, and so on. Each week all reported to the whole group, and again the group discussed the situation. Through this time of "speaking bitterness," the extent of past oppression became fully evident and any extortion of the past in rentals and forced gifts were all noted. The speaking of bitterness resulted in a psychological emancipation from the landed classes. It would be at this point that some of the more lurid events of violence took place, possibly through a mass trial, when many landlord families were virtually liquidated. As time passed a more moderate process of justice came to be the rule.

In the next stage, all the people in the land reform unit had to be assigned to their class category: landlords, reactionary or progressive; farmers, rich, middle, or poor; peasants, rich, middle, or poor. Again it was the group process. Each person started to assess his own position in this scale, and after he had suggested where he belonged the members of the group discussed his position with appropriate criticism and guidance.

Once the classification was done, the actual land division only awaited the compilation of all the resources that were to be shared, the land itself, the surplus furniture, the implements of production, and the farm animals. Those possessing more than a stated amount of any of these things surrendered the excess, and it was available for equal distribution among all claimants. This meant that nationally there might be considerable discrepancy from area to area, for when the people of a particular area were less numerous, the division meant larger portions than in a crowded region where only very small sections of land could be allotted. This was to prove a problem at a later period, and perhaps one factor in the speeding up of collectivization.

It is important to note that the phrase the "liquidation of the landlord class" did not necessarily mean the physical extinction of all landowners and their kin. Many did suffer death, where their own treatment of peasants had been ruthless or where the peasants went to extremes. On the whole, however, liquidation meant that landlords ceased to be members of the class, and, for those who were "progressive" and who remained on the land willing to till their own share like others, there was no further reprisal after the surrender of property and possessions.

The Korean War had broadened the need for an inclusive united front and in many areas the "rich farmers" were exempted from the category of a reactionary class.

The whole process of land reform became a sieve by which the people were sorted and tested. Any sympathy shown for the landlord, be it by the volunteer worker or the farmer, was regarded as a mark of old unenlightened thinking and so might be dangerous to the country. Many workers have earned a blighted reputation through showing "weak" sympathy with the sufferings of the oppressor class. Land reform not only served the ends of economic reform, but forwarded the ideological reorientation of the whole populace, as group after group took part in the program. The educated, confronted with the elemental burdens of the peasantry realized with a shock what the landlord system had meant. For the peasantry it was a new day.

The final celebration of the project for an area was a public and festive burning of the old deeds. New deeds were given out with little red flag markers for the new boundary lines through the fields, a reminder that all this blessing had come because of the Communist Party and the great leader and father of his people, Mao Tse-tung. So new minds were formed. True, the new taxes in rice were to prove as heavy, or even heavier, than that paid to the landlord before, but the taxes would no longer provide luxurious living for the landed family. They would support a great country, which would keep faith by setting up village schools and nursery education as soon as possible and in providing midwives and social services, which the country people had never before known. Here was a psychological revolution that was to make the commune not only possible but even potentially welcome. Land reform was not merely the satisfaction of the land hunger of the common peasant, it was also the seal of a revolution of mind and attitude.

Land Reform was completed by 1952. Collectivization was soon to follow. First mutual aid teams quickly demonstrated the advantage of a collective approach to the small land holdings, which had been all that the resources of land at the time of reform could provide. The land title was still held by the peasant. According to one source, payment to the government amounted to from 18 per cent to 27 per cent of the crop as tax, and surpluses could be marketed with the help of the co-operative agencies, which were, of course, also government controlled. It was a fact that the lot of the erstwhile poor peasants, or of those who had previously had no land, was significantly improved.

The low-grade producers' co-operatives were the next stage. Land was in effect pooled, though titles of ownership were still recognized. But the work of considerably larger units was done co-operatively, and even the decision as to what was to be planted in the fields under joint cultivation was a collective decision, with the government cadres naturally securing more and more influence in the situation. Return was in terms of the investment of each farmer, with ratios assessed, 30 per cent for land, 60 per cent for labor, and 10 per cent for equipment. Socialist trends here became very much more marked.

By 1955 the next step was taken. The government had been able to hold the loyal support of the great masses of the agricultural population, and it became advisable to proceed to collectivization to strengthen the total economy. Mao Tse-tung announced the program in July, and by November its promotion was going on apace.

Some observers claim that the peasants really pushed the transformation to communes beyond the government expectation or even ability to cope with the organization needed. Collectivization was established by 1957. In the "Great Leap Forward" of 1958, with the slogan of "twenty years in one day," the agricultural segment of society was making vast efforts to produce, produce, produce. The years 1959, 1960, and 1961 have certainly brought privation through natural disasters, and food shortages have been marked. It is difficult to know what the real situation is as the fact of famine becomes political grist for our Western press. China itself withholds admission of the presence of famine as a matter of pride. So human need and hunger, and natural and generous response to it, become strangled in political antipathies. Pride and self-respect generally do resent charity and prefer going hungry to accepting handouts.

The rural church has at no time had an easy life since the People's government came into power. There were the restrictions of the early years, and the prohibition of any public meetings before land reform. Then came the process of collectivization. Individual farmers had only brief and irregular periods of leisure and not much money.

Christian dedication cannot express itself in the old institutional forms in a commune. For instance, men and women workers in a commune receive two free days a month, but they will not necessarily fall on Sundays. Evenings are occupied with lectures and discussion groups. Thus corporate worship for the Christian community becomes very difficult. It may well be that Christians in China will discover new modes of witness, but they cannot be in the familiar patterns of the institutional church. As we think of this, let us remember that the tiny minority that the Christians represent in any of these vast communal structures means that they really cannot be exempt from work routines or from common disciplines. How can we understand to the point where we can really pray *with* these folk, and not just *for* or *at* them?

* * *

"Four Months in the Country," by Kiang Wen-han, Y.M.C.A. secretary, was published in *T'ien Feng* magazine of January 26, 1959:[6]

Towards the end of last August I was honored by being invited to serve on an investigating committee to study conditions in the country, and spent four months in a village near Shanghai. This was just at the time of setting up communes, and so I was not only able to see with my own eyes the Great Leap Forward in agricultural production, but also personally took part in the whole process of turning over from a co-operative to a commune. Here I wish to tell something of the outstanding impression I received from this experience.

1. Eating, Living and Working with the Farmers. Our investigation team lived in farm homes. There were communal dining halls, so we ate in these with the farm people while we were there.

Our plan was to divide our time equally between work in the fields and our investigation work. It was a good discipline for me. We of the intellectual class never did any manual labor in the old society, and even were inclined to despise those who did, and thus we were cut off from reality. Through the discipline of labor we are able to cultivate affection for workers, and thus change our own inner selves.

. . . .

2. Pull Both Ends, and Hold the Middle. It was the busy fall season when we arrived in the villages. In order to hasten production we adopted the method of pulling at both ends and holding the middle, encouraging the progressives to be still more progressive, and urging the half-way or backward people to catch up with the progressives.

. . . .

3. Government Leadership is the Key to Advance. My four months' experience convinced me that the key to the great advance made last year in agriculture was the leadership provided by the Government, and government leadership means direction by the Party. Our government today is closely bound up with the whole question of production, for it is only through increasing production that the life of the farmers can be bettered.

. . . .

4. The Farmers Welcome the Commune. It was the middle of September when we began to set up the commune organization. The farmers had already learned, through debate and discussion, that this was the most efficient form of organization for promoting the Great Leap Forward in production. The cooperatives were too small in scale and so the capital available to them was too little, and the use of labor and materials not flexible enough; this proved to be a hindrance to farm mechanization and electrification, large scale planting plans, the fighting of natural disasters, and large construction projects, such as canals, roads, local factories, specialized production, and large scale cultural projects. In order to lift farmers out of the poverty and backwardness of several thousand years, it was necessary to have a greatly increased production, especially to increase the cash return, and to develop rural industries, and for this a change in rural organization was necessary; this truth was already well known to the farmers.

. . . .

5. A concern not only with Production but also with Living. After the organization of the Commune, the villages universally carried out the plan of the Three Changes and the Four Small Changes. The Three Changes are: a military type of organization; looking on production as a battle; communal living.

Along with the Three Changes are the Four Small Changes, which are required to obviate the hindrances to women taking their part in the Three Changes. These are: the collectivization of children, the communization of eating, the specialization of night-soil collecting, and the organization of laundry and mending. These are necessary in order to liberate the labor of women.

The Party and the Government, besides being concerned to promote production, also pay attention to the living conditions of the people. They see to it that in the communal dining halls the food is sufficient, is hot, is hygienic, and as good as possible. The nurseries and kindergartens take good care of the children, and give them good teaching. The authorities insist that workers in agricultural production must be guaranteed their definite rest periods. At the time of their monthly periods women are exempted from heavy labor. Such concern for the life of the people, as shown by the Party and the Government, is something that China has never seen before.

. . . .

6. Free Food—A Great Accomplishment. . . . In the past farmers were paid according to their recorded days of labor, but now the system has been changed to take account of their skill, strength and general attitude toward labor, and to put them into different classes accordingly. So this system is still by its nature the socialistic one of "To each according to his work," rather than the communistic one of "To each according to his need."

. . . .

7. The Democratic Attitude of the Cadres. The first task of the investigation team was to investigate the prevalence of the "three airs" and the "five tempers" among the cadres, because when these exist they are a great hindrance to close relations between the Party and the People.

According to my four months' experience in the country, I can say that a democratic spirit among the cadres is a regular thing, and that the three airs and five tempers when they do occur are immediately reproved and corrected. First, they all, from the Committee Secretary to the important cadres of the larger, medium or smaller teams, live very simply, and have no bureaucratic airs. . . .

The Government's concern today is the best interests of the People, how to raise the living standards of the People. In all the meetings I attended, whether local, village or county, the chief subject of discussion was how to raise production; in production and the Great Leap Forward the cadres always take the lead.

. . . .

8. The True Liberation and Development of the Workers. A little over seven years ago I spent three months in the country on the Land Reform program. At the time we were carrying on a struggle with the feudalistic landlords, and giving the farmers a new place in government. This time in my four months in the country I have taken part in the great revolutionary step of setting up a commune. I have learned to appreciate the diligent and thrifty character of the farmers, and have personally witnessed their remarkable energy in increasing production. I fully realize that it is only under the correct leadership of the Party and Chairman Mao that the great mass of peasantry, ground down by several thousand years of oppression, could have emerged into a significant place in society. And I realize further that it is only through the establishment of communes that we can make the transition to a true communistic society according to the principle, "From each according to his ability, to each according to his need."

Thirty years ago I took part as a student in the Chinese Christian Student Movement. This Movement took as its standard, "Based on the Spirit of Jesus, let us create a youth organization, establish strong character, carry out a revolution, and plan for the liberation and development of the livelihood of the people." That empty dream was entirely in the realm of Reformism and since the Christianity of that day, in both finances and thinking, was under the control of imperialism, so no matter what kind of a "movement" we tried to initiate, we still remained in the diabolical clutches of imperialism.

But now since Liberation, the life of the mass of working people has been revolutionized under the leadership of the Communist Party, and has attained that "liberation and development" that we only talked about. The accomplishments of the Communist Party are not just in the material realm, but also in the humanistic. Their concern for production is also a concern for livelihood, for the purpose of the former is to raise the level of the latter. . . .

CHINA: A GREAT POWER

The new China! Revolutionary China, a China moving into vast new horizons, yet a China still conscious of her long history and imperial past. It is significant that the Communist Party chose the ancient capital of Peking as its center of administration, for here is the heartland of imperial China, the China that held the hegemony of Asia, as the tribute caravans came from the north and the east and the south, and even on occasion from the far west. On all important occasions today the people see impressive leaders from foreign countries again paying tribute to the new government.

The drive for great power status is fundamental to all policies of People's China today, both domestic and international. Thus, despite the famine in the summer of 1961, a significant money loan to Ghana was announced: a diplomatic action that was costly at home but gave prestige abroad. Claims for territorial sovereignty in Tibet are domestic issues to the Chinese, because for centuries this mountainous region has been under the hegemony of the Dragon throne. Modern methods of communication and the increased efficiency of the new rulers bring this authority much closer than it has ever been before. Whatever the Tibetans themselves feel about being Chinese, even the overseas and exiled Chinese people find it hard to understand why the Western press refers to the invasion or suppression of Tibet. For them it has always been assumed to be Chinese, and this is equally true of Taiwan.

Relations of the People's Republic with North Korea and Viet-Nam, which are in a sense her particular satellite states, are often intensified by rebuffs in other areas. Similarly aggressive actions may erupt in Chinese border regions, especially those which fall within the traditional historic influence of imperial days.

The fundamental force motivating Communist China's new role in international affairs is her militant nationalism. Once again it is essential to recall that for the first time since the decline of the Manchu dynasty the Communists have achieved unification in China. As a result of this unification, China has become the strongest and most assertive power in Asia. From the breeding-ground of international rivalries and exploitation, she has transformed herself into a centre of potent leadership.

This is the central fact one must bear in mind in approaching the problem of China. It is the expansive energy of the new regime seeking to assert its new power and position and its uncompromising challenge in advancing a new balance of power in the Far East that have produced the extreme tension in world affairs that we are witnessing.[7]

Not only is there a sense of history behind this new nation, but also a sense of unshakable destiny as it looks forward to the future. The Chinese Communists are determined to convince the world, especially their Asian neighbors, that the ultimate victory of the Communist cause is inevitable. They are convinced that history is on their side. It is this which gives the leadership the confidence and—sometimes—the frightening belligerence evident in their statements. The communication of this assurance of eventual triumph to their own people is a source of strength and inspires a willingness to undergo tremendous privation for the eventual glorious and triumphant future that is sure to come. Such motivation is continuous with the storied past. If these people of proud heritage do not satisfy the urge for great power status within the present international family of nations, they may make their claims felt in very intransigent fashion, or move back into the self-confident isolation they have known before. Echoes of such tendencies may be heard in Christian statements as well. For the church in China today sets itself to be fully Chinese, and in reaction to its foreign origins shows some of the exaggerations of a superpatriotism.

* * *

A letter from Christians of China to Christians of Hungary, written from Shanghai, May 24, 1957, was signed by some twenty well-known Christian leaders.[8]

DEAR BRETHREN IN CHRIST:

We twenty fellow-workers in the Chinese Church send to you and through you to all Christians of Hungary our warm greeting and brotherly love.

Since the tragic events of last October in your country we

have been deeply concerned about your life and the developments in your Church. In our prayers we constantly remember you.

Although we do not fully comprehend the real situation in your country yet, observing from a distance, we have a strong impression that your country is facing a critical decision, whether to be swallowed up by the reactionary movement with consequent chaos and war, or whether with the aid of other socialist countries you will preserve the foundations of the socialist system and earnestly strive to correct mistakes made in the past. We are delighted that you have chosen the second way. May God bless you and grant you abundant wisdom and strength.

In China we too have chosen the road of socialism. Our experience since the Liberation of 1949 clearly shows us that socialism means the elimination of poverty and exploitation. Moreover, it is only when the people themselves control the economic and cultural life of the nation that we can enjoy true freedom. . . .

During the past two years, relations between Chinese Christians and our Hungarian brethren have become more intimate. We have discovered the wealth of spiritual experience in your Church through these last twelve years. There are many things worth learning from you. Since we now live under the same kind of social order our theological thinking finds much in common. . . .

May the Holy Spirit be with the Christians in our two countries and enable us to bear faithful witness to Christ and his Gospel. We shall continue to remember you in our prayers.

Y. T. Wu speaks of "A Glorious Ten Years"—as he writes in *T'ien Feng,* September 21, 1959. This is part of a general account of China's progress in the first decade of the People's Republic:

After Liberation the Chinese Christian Church broke off the shackles of imperialism. In 1950 the Three-Self Patriotic Movement arose, which denounced imperialism, and severed relations with it, and this began a radical change in the Chinese Church. It was now no longer a tool to be used by foreign mission boards, but became a church under the control of patriotic and imperialism-hating Chinese Christians. This made a great change in the relations of Chinese Christians and the Chinese people.

The Three-Self Movement made Chinese Christians aware of the greatness and preciousness of their own country, made them realize that Christianity has been used as an imperialist tool, and opened their eyes to the glorious future of their own country. All of the great central Movements since Liberation, and especially those connected with the establishment of socialism, have educated and disciplined us Chinese Christians, so that we have determined to wipe out all traces of imperialist thinking and stand with the People, laboring on behalf of our country to establish socialism and preserve world peace.

. . . .

The past ten years have been glorious ones. . . . The great accomplishments of these years have stirred not only the Chinese people, but all people throughout the world who love peace and have a hope for the future. . . .

THE CHURCH AND THEOLOGICAL REFLECTIONS

The "Twenties"—Jesus the Democrat

"The missionary enterprise is the Christian campaign for international good will," said Harry Emerson Fosdick, well-known postwar liberal. This was the common conclusion. Democracy was a way of life as well as a political system, and it was the Christian way of life. Jesus, wrote the authors of a popular book on missions, was "the world's first and greatest democrat." It was Jesus, they said, who had introduced to mankind the infinite worth of every soul. From this had derived the concept of human rights. In hospitals around the globe missionaries, devoting their lives to caring for people of another race who were complete strangers, had demonstrated their belief in the sacredness of human personality. In schools in backward lands missionary teachers had lived out the principle of the dignity of man. The missionary movement was democracy at work. It was the force of the ideals of Christ, declared one writer, "that broke down slavery, that raised woman from the position of a chattel to that of a free being, that taught us to care for the sick, needy, and suffering, and that instilled the idea of human brotherhood."[9]

The "Fifties"—Jesus the Revolutionary

Early in the days of the new regime in China, a Christian apologetic for revolution was formulated which followed these general lines: Jesus was brought to the cross by the imperialism of Rome, the capitalism of the high priests, and the bureaucracy of the scribes. Imperialism, capitalism, and bureaucracy are the archenemies of the common people in China today, and hence are the major targets against which the revolution must work. Hence Jesus emerges as the great revolutionary hero, who gives his blessing on the essential causes of the People's revolution.

Apprehension

Christians in China had been very apprehensive as they faced the coming of the Communist regime, for the known atheism of the Communist, it was assumed, would bring privation and persecution. Most of us missionaries anticipated that our comparatively high standard of living would have to be surrendered. The Chinese Christian, on the other hand, was seldom a rich person. Each, however, had his own nervous anticipation and fears. All of us were probably fairly naïve about what was ahead for us, but we felt that God was leading us and we were ready to discover our obedience in the new China if we could.

During the period of the turnover, and especially in rural areas and small towns, churches were frequently occupied and regular worship ceased. Often the district official gave full rein to his own anti-Christian or antiforeign attitudes as ministers and Bible women met constant interference in their work and witness. Naturally in a period of testing, numbers drop off. There was a purging of the rolls, with all those who had trailed along in self-interest falling quietly away.

In many cities and towns, the church was the largest building available and hence it was in demand for the new mass meeting. As this building was usually used on Sundays but seldom during the week, refusal could certainly be misconstrued as not only a dog-in-the-manger but a reactionary attitude. So Chinese Christian leaders were very willing to open church buildings to gatherings of the "people."

Reassurance

The People's Political Consultative Conference, meeting in September of 1949, was in essence the nationally representative gathering that Sun Yat-sen had written into his blueprint for Chinese development toward democracy, but which the Kuomintang had postponed calling in any effective form while they extended the Period of Tutelage under one party. The conference nominated Mao Tse-tung as the President of the country and promulgated the Common Program and Organic Law, which was to be the operating basis for the People's Republic of China until a constitution was prepared. In the Common Program basic liberties were guaranteed to the people who fall into four classes: the peasants, the workers, the petty capitalists, and the national capitalists. The intellectuals, as the workers of the brain, were in the second classification. Freedoms were not accorded to the non-revolutionary classes.

The Constitution of 1954 confirmed these provisions, and the *China Handbook* summarizes these items as part of the basic contents of the constitution. The Constitution, says the *Handbook,*

> provided for freedom of speech, of the press, of assembly, association, procession and demonstration, and for freedom of religious belief. It declares that freedom of the person of citizens is inviolable. No citizen may be arrested except by decision of a people's court or with the sanction of a people's procuracy. The homes of citizens are also inviolable, and privacy of correspondence is protected by law. Citizens have the right to rest

and leisure, and to material assistance in old age, illness or disability.

Women have equal rights with men in all spheres of political, economic, cultural, social and domestic life, and the state protects marriage, the family, mother and child.

The Constitution not only guarantees these and other freedoms and rights but lays down that the state shall provide the necessary conditions to ensure that they can really enjoy them. . . .[10]

Among the representatives of the various elements and classes of people assembled in the 1949 People's Political Consultative Conference were seven persons representing religious groups. Two were Buddhist leaders and five were Protestant Christians. All were intellectuals with progressive attitudes. Muslim representatives were present too, but their category was that of a racial minority. The recognition of Christians in this initial conclave, called by the government, together with the guarantees of the Common Program, provided a new sense of confidence for the church. As time went by the church was to be proud of the many Christians who, as individuals or members of professional groups, were making their contribution to government activities from local to national levels.

Understandably the five Protestant representatives, following the conference, talked about the Common Program and basic policies developed there. They soon found themselves drawn as mediators into situations where local Communist or civil administrators were occupying church premises. The appeal to the provisions of the Common Program generally restored church property to its normal usage.

The National Christian Council met early in 1950 and discussed the church's contribution to the nation. The Szechwan Synod of the Church of Christ in China sent two delegates and I well remember their return. As these ministers reported on the council experience, they brought back a real sense of uplift and inspiration, and the two things they talked about were really a quiet comment on the past. For the first time in a national Chinese Christian gathering, all the speeches were in Chinese (no missionaries were present) and for the first time all denominations and groups in the church were included. As they pointed out it had taken the coming of the Communist regime to bring a comprehensive conference of Chinese Christians together!

At this time it was decided that the five Protestants who had been at the People's Political Consultative Conference should go with other leaders, making up teams that would inform Christians of their place in the new order and interpret the official policy regarding religion to officials and others in authority. Liaison with the government and interpretation were the order of the day, and regional conferences were held to help Christians reorient their thinking. The Chinese Association Press was already publishing small and easily comprehended books for the Christian reader on such titles as *The Biography of Mao Tse-tung, Dialectical Materialism,* and *The Democratic Dictatorship of the People,* along with other Marxist materials in such a way that Christian belief was also reinterpreted.

So it came about that teams of Christian leaders with the function of interpreting government-church relations began to travel here and there about the country. For was there not to be freedom of religion in China, along with freedom of antireligion? This meant that Christians could fully enjoy their rights to associate in church, read their Bibles in their own homes, and talk with friends who showed an interest. There was not to be freedom of proselytizing the unwilling, nor of street evangelism. This would be an offense to others and a denial of their freedom of unbelief, but the Christian could claim his own rights. There was an incident of the confiscation of a Bible from a pastor while on a journey by an over-zealous official who refused to return the volume though the pastor pointed out his constitutional right to possess and read it. The wronged Christian wrote to President Mao, and the Bible was returned with an appropriate apology from the offending official.

Korea

For us foreigners in 1949-1950, life was active and on the whole attitudes to us were very good. On the streets the wartime greeting of friendly approval was still heard—*"Ting hao,"* "Just tops!"—and sometimes to this was added the label of acceptance, "Soviet person."[11]

Our work with Chinese colleagues continued, although increasingly we kept to the background in any official encounters. A considerable group of missionaries had stayed into the new regime, believing that God's mission must be to all people. Some of us in Chengtu met weekly for a study group. This gathered a good cross-section of theological and political views, and we decided to work on the Marxist study documents which were then the focus of Chinese study. Thus we tried to follow the currents and thought trends which were affecting the Chinese, among them our fellow Christians.

It was about then that the Communist representative at the high school, where I continued to teach a few classes, explained the attitude of the new regime toward such staff members as ourselves. He explained to the students in assembly one day that there were foreigners and foreigners, and that we who were now teaching English in the school were "progressive." China, furthermore, would not make the same mistake that the Soviet had in banning religion. For it had not worked, and the policy had to be reversed during World War II in order to rally the Soviet people in the fight against Hitler. China would learn from the mistakes of her Soviet neighbor, and religion would not be persecuted, though, of course, the mature society would have no need of what was basically superstition. And so the foreign teachers were welcome in the school.

And then Korea! When news came over the Voice of America and the British Broadcasting Corporation that South Korea had been invaded, little did we know how much we would be affected by that news. For Korea was to bring a tough unity to China, rallying her people in a patriotic support of the government which would otherwise have taken years to achieve. It also made us foreigners "enemy aliens" as soon as People's China sent her troops into the field. This alien status was to cut us off from our Christian friends in somewhat the same way that Japanese Christians in Canada and the United States were isolated during World War II.

The first news in the Chinese papers in our part of the country followed the international broadcasts by a couple of days, which is of course quite in accord with the Communist philosophy of correct news release in contrast with the "scoop." The papers carried headlines about the invasion of the North Korean territories from the South, and in this American troops were shown to have taken a good deal of initiative. The news reports said further that the North, with its fighting preparedness and high morale, had been able to repulse the invaders; its troops were now already thirty miles south of the border. These initial releases caused little stir. It was almost as though with passive and unexpressive faces the Chinese put the paper aside and went on to talk of more immediate concerns. And so the propaganda line was not particularly persuasive. The war in Korea was a long way off, and what did it matter who had started it?

The weeks went by. The South Korean forces gained strength, and the armies under General Douglas MacArthur pushed northward. Finally in October of 1950, they were threatening the Chinese border as North Korean forces retreated into Manchuria. The bombing of the Yalu and threatening radio broadcasts from Japan regarding the aggressive intent of the advancing forces made it very easy for the Chinese press to blazen the violation of Chinese territory.

And by this time the Chinese troops were not only involved with fighting units in Korea, but the nation had come together with the cohesiveness of a clenched fist. No one, as was natural when the threat of invasion was deeply feared, bothered to engage in a considered discussion of rights and wrongs. The beloved Chinese land was being threatened by the foreigner again. It is a mistake to underestimate the force of the new patriotism, freshly discovered by many of China's ordinary folk and enforced through radio broadcasts, newspapers, and motion pictures.

The quality of support given the People's government in the Korean War may be illustrated by the special collections from Christians to purchase a fighter plane. It carried the name, "Church of Christ in China," and helped in the fighting in North Korea. So Christians responded as patriots.

I confess this memory followed me, in troubling fashion, and then one day in England I found a small church whose capital savings were all tied up in war bonds. In many churches colonial heroes are honored with plaques and flags as the nation's cause is commemorated over and over again.

The actual events and progress of the war need not concern us here, but perhaps enough has been said to indicate the importance of this development in consolidating the position of the People's government. Even those who had doubts about the new order were drawn into the new patriotism. China had become a clenched fist, united and strong. With this cementing of Chinese unity came a worsening of relations with the West, particularly with the United States. This was to affect the very heart of the Christian fellowship in China and caused many of us much troubled thought. Often it was difficult not to become bitter and resentful toward these trends.

The first straw in the wind, which most of us recognized with a shock, was the statement from the National Committee of the Y.W.C.A. after their annual meeting in March, 1950.

The statement needs to be read with a real effort to understand and not just to react with shock and hurt, which were our first reactions. This meeting of the Y.W.C.A. saw fit to terminate the employment of some secretaries from the West without any consideration of contracts or personal discomforts. (Part of this statement appears on page 68.)

Shortly afterwards one of the National Christian Council teams, visiting in Peking, asked for an interview with a government representative. They wished to clarify the position of the church and to know what the expectation of continued work and witness might be, especially with the encouragement of the freedom of religion clause in the Common Program. Premier Chou En-lai was very busy, so he met with the Christians on three different occasions in the middle of the night. One session ran from 2 to 4 A.M. A *British Weekly* article of July 10, 1952, recounts the tenor of the interview:

> The key-note of the conversations was struck by the Premier's saying that most or all of the difficulties which the Church was then experiencing stemmed from one root—prevalent doubts and suspicions regarding the Church entertained by officials and people alike, arising from the Church's entanglement with imperialism. The Church could find a solution to its various concrete problems only by making clear to all its complete dissociation from every imperialistic connection abroad, and the repudiation of all imperialistic elements within its own life. Past history was cited, beginning with the inclusion of clauses in the "Unequal Treaties" securing special facilities for the propagation of Christianity in China. The 1927 anti-Christian movement was represented as having been really a movement against foreign imperialism in the Church, rather than against Christianity itself. In the past, Christianity had, in fact, often shown itself progressive, but Christians must beware of "being used." Even when individual missionaries were free from direct political connections they were still unable to escape the influence of their upbringing and their imperialistic ways of thinking. Imperialism was defined as the use by one country of money or force to impose its own culture or trade upon another country so that it virtually became at least a semi-colony of the aggressive power.

The advocacy of "democratic individualism" by missionaries was given as further illustration of harm done to the Chinese people through the Christian Church. The Church must put its own house in order—and have no guests from abroad while it was in the process of so doing. Missionaries who were still in China might remain for the present, provided there were no suspicions of definite political activity, but only up to the time when they would normally return on furlough. The Church must become truly independent, self-supporting and self-propagating. It must give up its former non-political attitude, for politics were inseparable from the responsibilities of citizenship. Christians were called upon to show themselves truly patriotic, progressive and democratic. If they did this, they were assured they had nothing to fear.

It is easy to understand the importance of this conference. The line was to be drawn, not between what was Christian and what was Communist, but between what was foreign and what Chinese. Our discussion of the historic relations of China with Western nations may help us see why our Christian colleagues chose to stand for what was Chinese against what was foreign. And I think, in fairness to them, that they did so with real sincerity and a desire to co-operate with the government. For the evident accomplishments of the People's government in providing a stable administration, economic improvement and reconstruction, as well as the patriotic cause of the Korean War, had appealed to Christians as to other Chinese. Many experienced deepened loyalties as they took part in patriotic projects or national programs such as land reform.

A Christian Manifesto was written after the talk with the Premier, a conference in which a number of other Peking Christian leaders had also shared. In their eagerness and without extensive consultation with other Christians, they took the document back to Chou En-lai who received it with approbation, intimating that if this was in fact their sincere intent, there would be no question at all about the future of the church in China. Protestant Christians at the time did not number over six hundred thousand in a population thought then to number about five hundred million. Certainly it would seem that to the Premier the importance of the Protestant church was out of proportion to its statistical strength. When the manifesto was published, Peking papers hailed it with enthusiastic headlines, "Check Imperialist Plotting Activities! *Our* Christians Unite to Issue Statement." Originally the manifesto was to be something which Christians could opt to sign or not as they wished, but with the tightening of the whole pressured society through the period of the Korean War and the rounding up of the antirevolutionaries, it came to be a test not only of Christians as patriotic citizens and their support for the regime, but of political orthodoxy.

An Anglican countermanifesto echoes the loyalty to country expressed in the Peking document, but was phrased out of a context of much greater concern for the wider Christian fellowship, which was so sorely wounded in the first document. We could wish that zealous leaders at the beginning had submitted their statement to a wider Christian appraisal before taking it back to the Premier, for after he had seen it, alterations were very difficult. Many Chinese Christians signed because they were in favor of the main tenor of the manifesto, and it was far from clear whether their protest, if registered, would do the cause of reconciliation and a continued witness more damage than good.

Christian Manifesto

Protestant Christianity has been introduced to China for more than one hundred and forty years. During this period it has made a not unworthy contribution to Chinese society. Nevertheless, and this was most unfortunate, not long after Christianity's coming to China, imperialism started its activities here; and since the principal groups of missionaries who brought Christianity to China all came themselves from these imperialistic countries, Christianity consciously or unconsciously, directly or indirectly, became related with imperialism. Now that the Chinese revolution has achieved victory, these imperialistic countries will not rest passively content in face of this unprecedented historical fact in China. They will certainly seek to contrive by every means the destruction of what has actually been achieved; they may also make use of Christianity to forward their plot of stirring up internal dissension, and creating reactionary forces in this country. It is our purpose in publishing the following statement to heighten our vigilance against imperialism, to make known the clear political stand of Christians in New China, to hasten the building of a Chinese Church whose affairs are managed by the Chinese themselves, and to indicate the responsibilities which should be taken up by Christians throughout the whole country in national reconstruction in New China. We desire to call upon all Christians in the country to exert their best efforts in putting into effect the principles herein presented.

THE TASK IN GENERAL

Christian churches and organizations give thorough-going support to the "Common Political Platform," and under the leadership of the Government oppose imperialism, feudalism, and bureaucratic capitalism, and take part in the effort to build an independent, democratic, peaceable, unified, prosperous and powerful New China.

FUNDAMENTAL AIMS

(1) Christian churches and organizations in China should exert their utmost efforts, and employ effective methods, to make people in the Churches everywhere recognize clearly the evils which have been wrought in China by imperialism, recognize the fact that in the past imperialism has made use of Christianity, to purge imperialistic influences from within Christianity itself, and be vigilant against imperialism, and especially American imperialism, in its plot to use religion in fostering the growth of reactionary forces. At the same time, they should call upon them to participate in the movement opposing war and upholding peace, and teach them thoroughly to understand and support the Government's policy of agrarian reform.

(2) Christian churches and organizations in China should take effective measures to cultivate a patriotic and democratic spirit among their adherents in general, as well as a psychology of self-respect and self-reliance. The movement for autonomy, self-support and self-propagation hitherto promoted in the Chinese Church has already attained a measure of success. This movement from now onwards should complete its tasks within

the shortest possible period. At the same time, self-criticism should be advocated, all forms of Christian activity re-examined and readjusted, and thorough-going austerity measures adopted, so as to achieve the goals of a reformation in the Church.

CONCRETE METHODS

(1) All Christian Churches and organizations in China which are still relying upon foreign personnel and financial aid should work out concrete plans to realize within the shortest possible time their objective of self-reliance and rejuvenation.

(2) From now onwards, as regards their religious work, Christian Churches and organizations should lay emphasis upon a deeper understanding of the nature of Christianity itself, closer fellowship and unity among the various denominations, the cultivation of better leadership personnel, and reform in systems of Church organization. As regards their more general work, they should emphasize anti-imperialistic, anti-feudalistic and anti-bureaucratic-capitalistic education, together with such forms of service to the people as productive labor, teaching them to understand the New Era, cultural and recreational activities, literacy education, medical and public health work, and care of children.

The Korean War was to have far-reaching results in the Christian community. It meant the virtual end of missionary residence in China. This is not to suggest that, without Korea, we missionaries might still be working in China, but it did prove the immediate cause for withdrawal. It also started the Chinese church itself on a path which diverged sharply from that of their fellow Christians in the Western world. For us missionaries a combination of factors through 1951 made it impossible any longer to bring a useful contribution to Christian enterprises in China. Many of us came to be greater liabilities than assets.

Nationalization of Institutions

The freezing of Chinese assets in the United States brought prompt retaliation from the People's government: American funds in China were also frozen. This provided more material for propaganda to rouse anti-American feeling.

The freezing of American money in China meant that institutions depending on funds from groups in the United States were economically crippled and forced to appeal to the government for aid. By this time the national educational offices were well organized, and a special bureau was set up in the emergency situation for schools and other church institutions affected by the freezing of United States funds. This bureau acted in close association with the Religious Bureau in dealing with appeals. A conference was called in Peking in the fall of 1950 for the principals or heads of all institutions relying on American support. They were assured of government concern. And so in orderly fashion the great number of missionary schools became part of the national system. Often the new subsidies were larger than the old, which suggested the government's concern for quality and also implied the niggardliness of the foreigner.

As Canadians we were drawn into the process even though it was possible for our schools and hospitals to continue to draw their funds. But these institutions, sparked by the patriotic fervor of the day, held big meetings during which they repudiated the foreign money and, as patriotic children of China, returned to the "bosom of the ancestral land." So our money was no longer needed or wanted. Had this not been the case, it might have been even more awkward, as many of us reporting back to our mission boards and home churches would have had to say that the schools, in following national regulations and curricular requirements, were leaving little room for Christian activity. If funds were then cut off by Western churches, this might have led to even stronger political accusations, of having been willing to support schools under the reactionary Kuomintang program, but not under the educational development of People's China.

Thus, of its several streams of service and contribution, the Christian enterprise gradually lost control over all its institutions, medical and educational. The church was clearly not permitted to be involved in the social welfare of the country, although many of her sons and daughters were valued for their training and leadership. Their service now had to be rendered, however, within the context of primary loyalty to the regime. The church could continue to live, but for its worship and ritual life alone, not for its contribution to society, and its witness to the same society was carefully limited.

Alienation

The spring of 1951 brought a stepping up of the "Resist America—Help Korea" program. It also included a strong drive against the antirevolutionaries and spies, actual and potential, which easily expanded to a ferreting out of the foreign agents who might be hiding under the guise of religion, particularly in the Roman Catholic Church. We had weekly visits from the Foreign Office; the questions, friendly enough but formal and correct, seemed to be directed to discovering patterns of association within the foreign community. There were many queries about the amount of government support we had, and probably these well-indoctrinated officers never really believed that we were not connected with the Canadian government, or that American missionaries were supported by the free-will offerings of churches that did not consciously support a political objective.

During the Korean War, when the Central Committee of the World Council of Churches passed a motion of censure on the aggression by North Korea, Dr. T. C. Chao, one of the six vice presidents of the World Council, withdrew from the presidium of the world church body, and the link with the World Council was cut. We must remember that the Chinese church had received only information about aggression and violence against North Korea, so that their action here is not to be construed as simply a puppet echo of their government's policies. This was a genuine withdrawal from the West in terms of what they felt to be the true situation.

Christian statements and writings dating from this period do not make pleasant reading for us, but this does not mean that we should avoid the encounter, or dismiss the documents as biased or the result of internal pressure. If we draw on our knowledge of historic events, particularly that of the missionary connection with the hated unequal treaties and the more recent alignment of many Christians with the rulers of Kuomintang China, some understanding of the motivation may emerge.

The consequences of missionary involvement in "imperialism" broadly conceived are clear to us.[12] The lessons from China are multiple and salutary, a rewarding part of our search to understand what God says to us through the events of our time. Unequal treaties today are seen to be part of the exploitation of the nineteenth century, and it cannot be denied that missionary societies used the protection of these treaties to establish the church in China. Some students of the situation would say that without such protection the gospel could never have been preached in this ancient land, and it is difficult to contradict this statement entirely, though it is well to remind ourselves that God's power can never be permanently fettered by the conditions of men. An equally sound case can be made for the Chinese Protestant leaders who launched the manifesto, and for their colleagues who later became part of the patriotic Protestant church in the Three-Self Movement. Support of the government was the price of the life of the church in their view, not a betrayal of the Body of Christ, as it may rightly seem to the Western outsider looking on.

It was perhaps inevitable at this time that Christians would be troubled about many New Testament precepts. They accepted the injunctions of the Sermon on the Mount regarding the obligation to love one's enemy, and the contemporary stream of official hatred for the enemy was very difficult to counter. In this struggle of mind and heart there were both ideological and theological implications, and perhaps naturally there emerged a new exegesis, for example:

> "Love your enemies." When Jesus said this he was speaking to his disciples. The pronoun in the text is singular, and is the key to the passage. The enemy of whom Jesus speaks is a private enemy, not a public enemy. We must follow this truth in using love to overcome hatred for a private enemy, use gentleness to overcome violence. But as to the people's common enemies, rotters in the church, running dogs of imperialism, criminals who sabotage the revolution, shall we take that attitude? The answer is a plain, "No." If you hold a merciful view of these rotters it is as if you hid serpents in your bosom. The righteous God by no means requires that we love common enemies of the people like these.[14]

Does that shock you as it did me when I first heard it in People's China? Yet when I arrived back in my own country I found deep prejudice and resentment against anything remotely connected with Russia or communism. An objective attempt to interpret events in China or the Soviet brought down an accusation of being a "pink" or even more dangerously a "red." One certainly did not find that our citizens, members of the Christian church, were any more generous to their "enemies."

In April, 1951, the government called a conference of Protestant leaders, really to prod them in the promotion of the Christian Manifesto and to speed up the process of purging imperialist elements from the church body. To their surprise, the ministers present in Peking found that they were expected to accuse missionaries and their fellow Chinese who might be termed reactionary.

Undoubtedly many of the Christian leaders who were faced with the necessity of making this fateful decision would gladly have laid down their lives as martyrs for their Lord. The subtlety of the temptation is shown by the very fact that they succumbed. It did not appear to them that the point had been reached at which a stand must be made. Some of them no doubt convinced themselves that the course they felt compelled to take was actually in the true interests of the Christian community. One of these leaders wrote an account of the outcome of his night-long wrestling with the problem, and told how, before morning, "There came a great awakening." He experienced the pain of making accusations, but joy followed when it was over. He described the outcome in Christian terms as a "new birth." And he went on to advocate a thorough-going use of this method to purge the Church.[13]

Following this conference, the accusation technique was indeed used in the churches across the country. Very often those who fell under condemnation were missionaries who were either dead or safely out of the country, but one realized, as time went on, that the psychological effect of saying such things in criticism and accusation is itself a factor in destroying old ties and crippling present relationships as well. The church in China was to become a national church, but here was a severe strain on the wider fellowship. The most frequent charge was that missionaries had an "imperialist attitude"—and this was true, given the current understanding of the people. But the truth was exaggerated because of the offended pride and dignity of a Chinese people forced into an inferiority role through the past hundred years.

Missions were held to be imperialistic in organization, in finance policies, in their importation of foreign goods and materials instead of using what was available in China, and in alienating their converts from natural love of their own country. They were imperialistic in methods, and were certainly guilty of "cultural aggression."

Many missionaries had given generous financial help to individuals, students who became their protégés or to the families of their servants. They often left them such things as a rickshaw or a weaver's loom, thinking they could be turned to productive use. This practice was seen as an attempt to "buy the hearts" of the recipients. Missionaries were accused, along with other Western personnel, of "stealing

Chinese art treasures," and the extensive displays of Chinese embroideries, gowns of the Manchu days, pottery, and other treasures of this ancient culture which may be found in North American museums, give credence to this claim.

A good account of accusations may be found in *China: The Challenge,* written by Margaret Kiesow, who remained in China until December, 1954. At first her work was that of a missionary teacher in a Christian college; then later, after her marriage, she continued to lecture in chemistry in a government university. Her report of these years with its appraisal is very significant. Mrs. Kiesow writes as follows of the results of the accusation movement, as seen in a Christian college:

> After the accusation meetings many young people who had not known the discredited missionaries intimately, took the evidence at its face value, and accepted the official view that they were imperialist agents. Those who had known and loved the missionaries did not alter their former opinion, but they took good care to keep quiet about it in future. On the surface, the Communist-inspired campaign therefore succeeded and the personnel of the old Christian university went to their new jobs with all the latest Communist slogans on the tips of their tongues. They also went knowing that they must back up the slogans with a far greater keenness and responsibility for their work than many of them had shown before. . . .[15]

With the prodding of the government Religious Affairs Bureau a series of accusation meetings were held all over China. The churches previously linked with the National Christian Council were those most strongly drawn into this emphasis. By this time the Anglican leaders had pretty much fallen into line, and the more moderate terms of their version of the manifesto gave way to the more official document. Again we should not assume that the pressures were simply external. Even as an alien, labeled by my students as an "international and cultural spy," I experienced something of the magnetism of the mass movement which was the awakened

China. So much energy and enthusiasm were released and there was so much potential for good that it was very human to want to be part of it, even though aware of glaring defects.

So we may see the co-operation of Christian groups with government programs as a natural development, although it was marked by what seems to us betrayal of our friendship and service to them. In this co-operation there were the zealous and the enthusiastic, and there were others who moved reluctantly in the accepted patterns, and again others who, busy at their work, regretted the time spent on this "one more series of meetings" in a program where hours of each week had to be spent in political study. The Three-Self Movement, stressing self-propagation, self-support, and self-government for the church, gained increased influence and has become the group which provides liaison with the government Religious Affairs Bureau.

From essays on "Freedom Through Truth" by Y. T. Wu, the leader of the Three-Self Reform Movement, comes this concluding paragraph:

> Since liberation we frequently hear Christians saying, "Has Christianity any future?" That is a strange question to be upon the lips of Christians. What has happened to our Christian faith? Do we believe that the eternal God who made the heaven and earth exists today and will not exist tomorrow? Have we forgotten that the Christ whose life was full of mercy and truth is the same yesterday, today and forever? Do we believe that the Holy Spirit who has hitherto enlightened and guided our hearts, will now suddenly stop working? Not so. The eternal Triune God does not change with the times. It is not the faithfulness of God that we need be concerned about, but our own faithfulness. If we have deeds to match our faith, if we make an effective witness for Jesus Christ, then all our anxieties will be found to have been needless.[16]

The following patriotic resolutions grew out of the Three-Self Meeting of 1957 in Peking. This was published in *T'ien Feng* of March 31, 1958.

The Yuling District resolutions follow an introduction, in

which they state that in the present great leap forward in socialization they, as Christian pastors, are not willing to lag behind. They make the following guarantees:

1. We will observe the five don'ts, the five musts, the five loves and the five excellences. The five don'ts are: We will not break the laws, we will not preach reactionary doctrine, we will not try to get people to become Christians on the plea that Christ can heal the sick, we will not invite free-lance evangelists to preach in our churches, we will not attend or preach in underground services in homes.

The five musts are: We must cooperate in the government's religious policy, we must expose free-lance evangelists and underground home services, we must be economical, we must discipline our bodies, we must take part in every socialist campaign.

The five loves are: Love the country, the party, socialism, the Three-Self Movement, and labor.

The five excellences are: To improve in the openness of our thinking (through criticism and self-criticism), to improve in self-reform (by destroying capitalism and establishing socialism), to improve in mutual respect (that is, between believers in different faiths, or between believers and non-believers), to improve in political study.

2. Besides our personal strengthening of our own political studies as pastors, we will also organize study classes for our laymen in every church.

3. We will answer the call of the government in regard to public hygiene, and in every church strictly obey the six don'ts and the three cleansings.

4. We will heed the call of the government in regard to birth control, not only in our own families, but recommending it also to our laymen.

5. Every church will plant trees in every available place on its land.

6. We will wipe out illiteracy in all church members between the ages of 14 and 40 during the year 1958.

7. Any church members that have come to Shanghai from outside villages, we guarantee that we will mobilize them 100% to return to agricultural production.

8. Before the May 1 celebration, the preachers will learn six patriotic songs to use in the parade.

9. We guarantee to mobilize at least 85% of our church members to participate in every social campaign.

10. We preachers guarantee to take part in the savings program (with exception of those in particularly difficult circumstances) and to urge it upon our church members.

11. Once a quarter we will have a criticism meeting on the above points, commending those who have done well, and criticizing those who have not.[17]

ISOLATION: THE GREAT WALL OF CHINA

A verse from a Liberation Song:

> Arise, you who refuse to be slaves,
> Our very flesh and blood will build a new Great Wall.
> A savage indignation fills us now,
> Arise, arise, arise![18]

The People's Republic of China is a new nation, unified as it has never before been unified. And this tempered-steel unity has only been strengthened by the isolation into which the proud nation has been placed by the Western countries. The Chinese Communist Party leadership and indeed the whole people have been deeply affronted not only by nonrecognition but by the international fiction that Chiang Kaishek and the Taiwan regime are China.

Whatever may be the objective ethical view, the so-called moral argument against recognition so strongly advanced by conservatives, political or Christian, is a particular annoyance to Chinese pride and sensibility. This is not hard to understand if we make even a tentative imaginary effort to "sit where they sit." The Chinese Christian is, if anything, more sensitive in this regard than his fellow nationals, perhaps because of the paternalism and patronizing benevolence many have personally experienced. In actual fact incidents of such a nature may have been very minor in their lives. But the pressures of antiforeign, particularly anti-American, policies in China and the continuing condemnation of Chinese communism by Western Christians—who, they feel, have made little effort to understand the Christian Chinese who remains a patriot, or to respect his sincerity—both combine to keep bitter memory alive and to feed current resentments. All of us are then caught in mutual recrimination and moral condemnations, hardly worthy of our Christian heritage. Yet on both sides the name of Christ and the cause of righteousness becomes the justification for our mutually intransigent positions. Of course, if we are right, then our position is secure. But are we, in all honesty, completely right?

Chinese patriotism and ideological self-consciousness have been so nurtured that the story of "imperialist aggression" over all of Asia and the debilitating administration of colonies have remained unhealed wounds in the body of world relationships. The events of the last decade have been as salt, stinging smartly when rubbed into the open sore of bitter memory.

Isolation, which to begin with was imposed by the outside world's ignoring the new regime and passing her by, now has become aloofness, chosen by the Chinese nation itself. And here again is an echo of the dynastic eras when the Middle Kingdom kept apart from the barbarian world without, protected by the buffer of geographic barriers. Today the isolation of a more profoundly dividing barrier is one of attitude, arrogant as of old, but hurt too. It is connected with the nation's normal pride and desire to be, not only in fact but in the consciousness of the whole world, a great power.

The sheer number of China's population, more than a quarter of the human family, combines with the sense of destiny to make China very confident in her historic and ultimate triumph. China, alone among the powers, does not need to fear atomic war. She can be fairly certain that if and when other nations have been wiped out, many of her people will remain, for it is impossible to annihilate all of China, land or people. And in her present increasingly intransigent mood, she is willing to make considerable sacrifices. Her people are expendable, perhaps in a fashion which is deeply offensive to us.

The Korean War launched the hate-America campaign, and it is appalling to realize how constantly this record has been played ever since. The United States has become the archfiend and prototype of threat and evil for the Chinese—just as communism is the bogey for so many of our population. In a recent speech given by a Chinese leader at an international conference, reference was made to "American warships on the Yangtze River," when in point of fact the offender of the days under discussion was Great Britain. All of the brunt of the hundred years of unequal treaties must now be borne by the nation that came latest of all to Asia, and then with perhaps less oppressiveness than the others. In 1953 Mrs. Kiesow, who resided until that time as a university teacher in Peking, summarized attitudes which she sensed among her associates and in the Chinese press.

> . . . Readers will find that the arch-enemy is the U.S.A. All other Western countries, including Great Britain are just her satellites. The U.S.A. is represented as a great Fascist power, directly or indirectly responsible for all the evils which exist in the non-Communist world, particular emphasis being laid on South America, Africa and the Near East. She, or her chief satellite, Great Britain, can always be relied on to do her best to squash any movement for national sovereignty or the assertion of human rights anywhere, and to do it with the utmost possible cruelty and inhumanity. Even the gifts and loans are only an outlet for American big business, and a means of keeping other peoples in economic as well as in political slavery. The American and British people are not completely identified with all this. They are represented as ground down in poverty and hardship by the armaments race engineered by the big business men who control the governments. Their minds are, however, poisoned by films of gangsterism, guns and sex, while their children are led astray by similar stories in comics, and by an educational system which teaches competition and individualism instead of co-operation and concern for the public weal. In addition, they all

live in daily terror of the H-bomb. The Soviet Union and the other People's Democracies are, of course, the complete antithesis of all this. They are the camp of peace and reconstruction where all children can look forward to a happy future. When it is realized that Christians in China have read and discussed, but could not openly disagree with, newspaper articles in this strain nearly every day of the week for several years, no surprise will any longer be felt at letters and articles which they write for foreign consumption.[19]

A more recent writer, Tibor Mende, in the book, *China and Her Shadow,* points out that 170,000,000 have been born since the People's Republic of China was established, and some two hundred million more have come to mental maturity. The figures approximate the total North American population. Mende discusses the awareness of all China's people of the real achievements of the regime in maintaining order, eliminating corruption, controlling disease and famine, and providing full employment for her people. It has been at great cost, but perhaps we are more troubled about the price involved in all these positive results than are the Chinese themselves!

The people of China also know of the efforts made by Western nations to prop up the previous government of Chiang, when he had quite evidently lost the "mandate of heaven" as it were, and of the refusal by this same group of nations to grant China her rightful place in the councils of nations. So they feel that there is a determined effort to discount the real achievements of the new regime. For them their increased military power is a guarantee against further humiliation at the hands of the West, and they would be surprised to think that their armed might appears in as threatening guise to others, as it actually does, just as we are offended when the farflung defense bases for our own protective organization are termed by the Asian to be a threat and a symbol of aggressive intent. So with the failure of the West to appreciate the attitudes of China, and the intransigent and threatening gestures of China toward us, there is the building up of what Tibor Mende terms a new Great Wall, a wall of mental separation. The Bamboo Curtain has thickened, and with a new self-centeredness it is no longer a curtain, but a sturdy wall of alienation. China is withdrawing into self-containment and pride.

Surely for us this means that we must make an effort to perceive how this unfortunate situation has come about, and be ready for the long and laborious process of becoming informed about China and doing what we can for the process of mutual understanding. A moral platform of superior righteousness from which we pass easy judgment will bear no fruit in communication, not to speak of the reconciliation which the world so badly needs. Nor will there be the renewal of conversation with our Christian brothers for which we yearn, but for which they seem no longer to have any desire.

* * *

The following is a speech delivered by Bishop K. H. Ting at the All-Christian Peace Assembly in Prague, Czechoslovakia, June of 1961:

DEAR BROTHERS AND SISTERS IN CHRIST,

We Christians of many countries thank God for this opportunity to assemble here to discuss the issues of world peace. It is God who has called us together to be His instruments in the accomplishment of His will. At the same time, we are keenly aware not only of the eager hopes which peace-loving people everywhere place in our endeavors, but also the support Christians all over the world are giving us through their prayers. This impresses upon us the immense responsibilities we bear as we meet. The Church leaders in China are much concerned about the role of Christians for safeguarding world peace, and ask us to convey to you the very cordial greetings and the high hopes for peace of the Chinese people and of Chinese Christians. We should like to mention particularly that for the cause of peace, the Government and people of Czechoslovakia have given much help to the successful convocation of this assembly. . . .

The defense of peace is a momentous issue of universal concern in the present-day world. In our generation, war and aggression have taken away the lives of millions of people, and now, we are confronted with the menace of new war. As pastors, we are concerned also with the fact that the atmosphere of war is corrupting the moral and spiritual quality of some people. Some friends from the West have told us that international tension has made a number of intellectuals in their countries to think that life is meaningless, since war might start tomorrow. Since there is no assurance as to personal security, they say, let us eat, drink and be merry, for tomorrow we die. All long-term planning for one's life and all moral considerations have become unnecessary. The atmosphere of war is degenerating their spirits and making them selfish. They become depressed and disillusioned, and are without altruistic ideals or any sense of responsibility for upright living. . . .

Dear brothers, the mission of the Church in the world is the offering of worship on behalf of man and the bearing of witness to man. If the human soul is captivated by this cynical view of life, he cannot take any attitude towards all goodness, honesty, conviction and idealism except that of contempt and scorn. And this is exactly the great obstacle the Church is facing in its efforts to guide man to see the validity of worship and witness. . . .

. . . Nevertheless, in the propaganda of some countries, aggression is referred to as "defending freedom," the plunder of natural resources and exploitation of the cheap labor of the colonial peoples as "giving aid." They slander the national liberation movement of Asia, Africa and Latin America as "communist aggression." As such, a small group of neo-colonialists is tramping upon the reason and conscience of man. They are not only toying with words of peace with their lips, but also exploiting the conscientious aspirations of millions and millions of people.

Brothers and sisters, we hold the Gospel most precious, but the bellicose elements on the other side of the Atlantic Ocean have even come to utilize the Christian religion for the implementation of its policy of war and aggression. Because of this abuse, there are even clergymen who have become war propagandists. . . . But the small handful of war-makers are not the real masters of history. The fate and destiny of billions of people is not doomed to be tramped upon. If we probe the issues of the present-day world with a deeper perspective, we see that the era in which a small handful of war-makers can exploit the people unscrupulously has gone.

Dear brothers and sisters, Professor Hromadka has rightly stated in his address that "Mankind is going through a process of changes which are unprecedented in history." The hallmark of our epoch is the awakening of the peoples of the whole world. From the Elbe to the Pacific, one third of mankind is already building a new pattern of society according to the ideals of socialism. In Asia, Africa and Latin America one and a half billion people have gained their national independence since the second world war. In South Korea, South Vietnam, Turkey and other areas, people have arisen again and again to fight neo-colonialism of the U.S. Government, and to strive for a life of independence and freedom in accordance with their own wishes. From the Caribbean Sea to Iceland, from Tokyo Bay to Iraq, there is an upsurge of the just struggle against new-colonialism. In Western Europe and North America, an ever increasing number of people, including the people and Christians of U.S.A., are taking actions against nuclear weapons, arms expansion and war preparations. We, peoples of various countries, all love peace ardently in spite of the differences among us. We all advocate peaceful co-existence among countries of different social systems, friendly intercourse of peoples and economic and cultural exchanges. On these broad bases, the peoples of various countries are rallying together ever more closely.

These and other facts indicate that the people's movements of national independence, freedom and peace form the main current in the development of history. Today, there are many church leaders and members on the five continents who join hands with the vast bulk of people and are actively taking . . . their share of responsibility in these movements. We Christians have our own faith. But Christ has not asked us to isolate ourselves from the world, the Christ who is risen and now sits at the right hand of God is not only the Lord of the Church but also the Lord of the world. The secular movements of the people have important significance. What man achieves in history is finally not to be negated or destroyed but, in the new heaven and new earth, will be received in Christ and transfigured. In this respect, Christ has set for us an example: for the sake of reconciliation between God and man, He "emptied Himself" and came into human world "taking the form of a servant." He identified himself with humanity "made like unto his brethren in every respect," Christ, as the Priest of the New Covenant after the order of Melchizedek, is different from all human priests precisely in the very thoroughness of his identification with man, with man's aspirations, cravings, and strivings from the depth of their hearts. If the Church is to be loyal to its Lord and fulfill its priestly function, it must learn the lesson to love their people and stand by them.

Throughout these years, God has taught us Chinese Christians to look at the changes of our country with such an attitude. . . .

For a full century, China fell into the status of a semi-colonial country. In those days, battleships flying the Stars and Stripes bristled threateningly on the Yangtze River. U.S. made commodities were dumped in China strangling our national industry and agriculture. Under the reactionary rule of the U.S. servant Chiang Kai-shek, the Chinese people were plunged into an abyss of incredible suffering. Everywhere you would find beggary, robbery, theft, prostitution, disease and cesspools of filth and crime. The conscience of Christians was being tortured; the Church of Christ was also plagued by evils and crimes. But, our people, rallying together in close ranks, after protracted and arduous struggles and with the support of the peoples all over the world, eventually drove out the U.S. imperialism and its tool Chiang Kai-shek, and won victory in 1949. For the first time in history, the people themselves became the master of their country. The people now have a good Government of their own. The wisdom and strength of the people and the rich natural resources of our country are no longer subject to the exploitation of the imperialists, but are used to give well-being and happy life to the people.

A great and lofty ideal has pulled the six hundred and fifty million Chinese people closely together. The enthusiasm and creative labor of the people is gradually changing the backward China into a country of highly developed modern industry, agriculture, science and culture. Today the livelihood and employment of the people are ensured. Life becomes very meaningful. A new moral standard of "one for all and all for one" has formed up, and is prevalent in our whole society. Beggary, robbery, prostitution, gambling, and all other kinds of vices and evils have been done away with forever. The freedom of religious belief is guaranteed by Law. The Church and believers carry on their worship and witness in joy. For all these, Chinese Christians are filled with thanksgiving, for God has listened to our prayers in these years. We offer our thanksgiving and praise before the throne of God, and receive power from above to purify our Church in China and to realize self-administration, self-support, and self-propagation in the Church. In this way, we shall be able to live to the glory of God and with the rest of the Chinese people to build a more prosperous new China. We need peace. Therefore, we vigorously join our efforts with those of other peoples to defend peace and eliminate aggression. Chinese Christians and Chinese people take note with gladness that the will of the people is fully manifested in the foreign policy of peace. It strives for the peaceful co-existence of countries of different social systems. It supports the various peace proposals of the Soviet Union and other peace-loving countries. Our Government has time and again proposed that countries of the Pacific region, including the United States, conclude a peace pact of mutual nonaggression and that the Pacific region be made an area free of nuclear weapons. The past year presents striking examples. The border question between China and Burma and between China and Nepal have both been satisfactorily settled through friendly negotiation. We have signed friendship and nonaggression treaties with many countries. And even towards the U.S. Government, despite its aggression against China and its continued occupation of China's territory Taiwan, our Government still sits down with great patience to negotiate with it, in the quest for a peaceful solution of the disputes between China and the U.S.

In the light of people's own experiences, we extend sympathy and support to the national liberation movement of Asia, Africa, and Latin America. From these continents, in the repeated struggles of their peoples and through the talks of brothers and sisters of these continents present at this assembly, we hear the words which God said to Moses on the mountain of Horeb, "I have seen the affliction of my people who are in Egypt, and have heard their cry because of their taskmasters: I know their sufferings, and I have come down to deliver them." The love and mercy of God and the voices of men from these continents not only impel us to give them full support, but also lead us to the firm conviction that their just cause to unshackle the yoke of neo-colonialism will achieve ever greater victories. Peace cannot be separated from justice. The victory of the struggle against colonialism is the victory of the cause of peace.

Dear brothers and sisters, the contemporary epoch is characterized by the awakening of the people and their struggle for independence, freedom and peaceful co-existence. Only a small handful of warmongers over the other side of the Atlantic Ocean are against peace. Today, they become ever more isolated. The forces of peace surpass those of war. But in spite of this peace will not come by itself. Peace must be won. Our question then is how to win peace.

We all remember, particularly our friends from Europe, that in the 30's the policy of appeasement pursued by the then Prime Minister of Britain Neville Chamberlain had not prevented Hitler's aggression over Europe; on the contrary, it facilitated the launching of the second World War by Hitler. The peoples of China and other Asian countries also remember that in the 30's, Chiang Kai-shek adopted the policy of non-resistance against Japanese militarism, the result of which was Japan's all-out aggression, of China, and later, of the whole of Southeast Asia. Today, in the 60's, a recent striking example is that the Cuban people in close unity and with the support of the whole world, have defeated the massive invasion of U.S. mercenary troops. The historical and contemporary lessons have told us that we cannot attain peace through appeasement of the aggressor. Peace can be safeguarded only by relying upon the united efforts of the peoples of the whole world.

Brothers and sisters, let us discern in the people's movement for peace and for national independence the loving hand of God, so that we may know that it will surely win and may participate in it and find in it the path of our common obedience. In doing so, it is not impending death or the fear of death that is driving us, but the love of man, the rendering to God of our services and to Christ our adoration, the sanctification of the Church and the strengthening of its witness. Let us dedicate our hearts and minds anew in the prayerful words of *Theologica Germanica:* "I would fain be to the Eternal Goodness what his own hand is to a man."

6 · *Conversation Among Christians*

A Letter from Soochow, September, 1959[1]

At first glance it would seem that the church in China has no hope. But in fact the opposite is the case. We who believe in God also believe that all the vicissitudes of life are governed by God. He will fulfill His will and raise up a united church, which is what our Lord prayed for. Just as God long ago used Cyrus, so today He is using Chairman Mao to cleanse His church. He will raise up a church which will not be the church of any one person but of all believing people.

In this transitional period the church is daily growing stronger. This is the work of the Holy Spirit, by Whose influence the faith of believers is being united. At first Soochow had only one place of worship but recently because of the increase in the number of worshippers it has been necessary to open a second place of worship—one has its service in the morning and the other in the afternoon. In the future still more places of worship may be opened as need arises.

We must remember that the Lord Jesus Christ is the true God, and that the human heart needs its faith. Our Lord has said that heaven and earth may pass away, but His word will never change. And so I believe that His church on earth will grow and prosper.

It is time to draw the threads of this story together. Servants of God continue to bear their witness as members of the Church, the Body of Christ in People's China. We have seen how the institutional church which moved into the Communist society has been broken, and molded and changed. We have tried to understand the motivation which has made the adjustment to Chinese society under communism so complete, as the church has become part and parcel of the new nation, and has apparently endorsed government policies without reserve. From the days of the Manifesto and Accusation movements on, the leaders of the Three-Self Movement have increasingly led the way in the conferences and policy-determining activities of the Chinese church. The communalization in both rural and urban areas has seriously influenced the whole pattern of church activities as individual incomes lessen with the resulting inability to give towards a minister's salary. So the professional servants of the church have had to take part in productive enterprises. There seems also to be a strong move toward church unity in China today, which is reported as bubbling from the membership of the local church, as well as being encouraged from its leadership. Christian leaders in China do not seem to feel that this trend has been in any way forced on them by government pressures. There is no doubt about the continued vitality of the worship of the church in China today, though the expression of its thanksgiving may come to us in terms that are hard to reconcile with many of our own ideas. Perhaps we should not try to "reconcile" what we feel honestly denies the essence of God's revelation, but surely it is "of the Spirit" to try to understand even such a rationale.

In 1959 the church celebrated the ten years of liberation, and in *T'ien Feng* there were many articles on this occasion. One is by the Rev. Cheng Hsi-san, a Methodist of Tientsin.

He describes himself as "an old man of over sixty, who has seen many governmental changes, and has in the past cherished many illusions, only to have them destroyed. The bitter taste of the old China is something which the young man in China today can hardly understand." He goes on to speak of the way in which the Christian Church has thrown itself whole-heartedly in the Great

Leap Forward, and says, "Last year, when the whole country was making its Great Leap Forward, we church workers on the basis of an awakened understanding took part in the Movement. What a glorious thing it was when we found ourselves at one with the workers of China, how happy we were to find that we could be fellow-workers in the building up of a socialist China.

"On Sunday when we went to the house of God, our hearts naturally raised themselves in praise to God saying, 'Lord, Thou art near to us and wholly living within our hearts.' For then we realized that all the sale of sheep and cattle and doves and the putting on of sheepskins by wolves, had been purged from our temples, and so we were able to say, 'How happy it is for brethren to be able to dwell together in unity.' "[2]

For a much more adequate account of the church itself in today's China the reader is referred to *The Church in Communist China* by Francis Price Jones. In his concluding chapter are these words:

. . . . Something of a modus vivendi has been arrived at between Protestant Christianity and the Chinese Communist party. The latter, so far, is willing to recognize the former, and guarantees a certain degree of freedom of religious belief, on the condition that Chinese Christians show themselves loyal citizens and co-operate in the establishment of a new economic order.

These conditions of acceptance and co-operation are not in themselves necessarily subversive of the principles of Christian liberty. Throughout the two thousand years of church history, many a Christian has exhibited loyalty to a government no more deserving of it than the People's Republic of China and has worked through and supported a variety of economic systems. It is therefore understandable that most Christian leaders in China have accepted these conditions, and that the Christian church has in consequence received government recognition and been accorded a modest niche in Chinese society, so that it has not been compelled to go underground.[3]

The church then has come to terms with the society in which it finds itself. One is tempted to say it has become "domesticated"—domesticated in a greater degree, but in the same sense perhaps that the upper middle class churches of

Canada and the United States reflect their milieu and culture, and as part of the pattern of life do offer shepherding and nurture to the faithful and instruction for inquirers. But the prophet finds himself an alien. Certain it is that the Christians in China today see their service within the framework of the Communist ideology dominant in that land today, and do not feel that they are any the less believers, or that they have compromised their loyalty to their Lord and Savior.

A visitor to Peking in the summer of 1960 questioned a Y.W.C.A. secretary regarding the Christian aim and purpose of that association. The reply was:

> The Y.W.C.A. is a body in the service of society. The needs of our members and the needs of society are not contradictory. The ideology of the Y.W.C.A. is different from the atheism of Communism—but this is not the key point. We feel the important thing is that the fate of all Chinese people is the same—we all suffered the same under the Japanese and under Kuomintang corruption. We all aspire the same today to peace and prosperity. The Y.W.C.A. is different today than it was before Liberation—it is really Chinese. You must remember Christianity was introduced to China by foreigners—now since Liberation, the Y.W.C.A. (and the Christian Church) is really our peoples', not managed or controlled by outsiders. It was a liberation of the Y.W.C.A. as well as for the nation.[4]

The official pronouncements of the church as well as many individual testimonials show gratitude for the Government's implementation of the constitutional right of religious freedom. But there has never been any modification of the avowed atheism of the Communist leadership or of the assumption that religion will someday have served its purpose and be left behind by a truly progressive society. This means that the serving of God in a Marxist land has its own particular context of challenge and faithfulness, and the hands of the Christians will be strengthened with our understanding of this situation. Can we learn how to support them, rather than contributing on our part to the deepening alienation that brings into the Christian fraternity the tensions of the cold war? Those whom we call servants of God see their hard-working Marxist fellows as other servants of God who do his will even though not offering him either recognition or fealty.

What of the relations between the Church in China and the Church in the West? Can there be conversations? Or is the new Great Wall thickening for us too? There is no space here to detail the degree of contact that there has been through the period of the last decade. Since the major missionary withdrawal in 1950 and 1951 there have been a few channels of personal information. Occasionally an imprisoned missionary or foreigner after serving his or her sentence has brought this story to the outside world. A few, like Nancy and Ralph Lapwood and Mrs. Kiesow, remaining in teaching positions, have given us helpful insights.[5]

There have been delegations composed either of church folk or including Christians, who have brought reports of the ongoing life of the country. Along with the extensive documentation of such groups there are many reports available from individual business men, travelers, and reporters, holding citizenship other than that of the United States. Some have been most favorably impressed, others have only seen the other side of the coin, and still others have struggled to weigh the merits and demerits with some kind of generosity. And each of us reads these reports with his own approach, his own predilections, his own readiness or reluctance to be open to a point of view different from his own.

As our Chinese fellow Christians remind us again and again in their pronouncements, the faith was taken to China by missionaries, who were inextricably bound up with imperialism. The breaking of this connection was the first task undertaken by the progressive arm of the Chinese church as we have seen, and we need to remember it was not only the government who approved the end of foreign connections for the church. The Chinese Christian was glad of the new independence which was now his, as the indigenous church really felt that it ruled in its own house. It is tragic to think that gratitude for this new independence is appropriately accorded to the Communist Government and not to the generosity and support of the wider Christian community; which did and does, after all, pay lip service at least to the idea of national and independent churches. Perhaps we can understand why the acclaim for the government policy has also exaggerated the offenses of the Western church and soft-pedalled the points of real Christian contribution. It is also a natural reaction that the church in China would turn to its own responsibility within the borders of China, seeing this as a new priority, while feeling that the loss of ties with the West may not be as tragic as it seems to many of us. Often adverse reports of the church in China given to the American people result in further Chinese withdrawal, and the reinforcement of the opinion of Chinese Christians that we of the West have no capacity to appreciate what is happening. The report of the visit of the British Quakers is helpful to us here.

> The China Christian Three-Self Patriotic Church claims to fulfill both loyalties [to the government and to the church]. "Why should we want to be against the government?" exclaimed a young Anglican priest, and went on to say that it was not hard to be a patriot when patriotism meant working for the fulfilment of so much that the Church has always worked for. Other Christians told us of their conviction that the Church has a definite place in the revolution. It is possible that the government shares their view. The moral demands of Christianity and the moral demands of Communism run parallel up to a point, and the activities of the Church may even be welcomed so long as they are seen to help towards the making of good citizens. By the same token the inflexible Papal allegiance of the Catholics is inconvenient and obstructive and cannot be tolerated. The real difficulty will come for the Protestant Church if and when at some future date patriotism is no longer enough, when the demand will be for a more fundamental acceptance of the theoretical foundation of Communism. . . .

It has already been said that one facet of the new patriotic conscience of the Churches is the ending of all dependence on the Church in the West, and a great pride in this new independence. "The missionary era is over. It is now the duty of us Chinese Christians to preach Jesus Christ in China and bear witness to Him among our own people." Since the blocking of most of the channels through which their outward and social testimony flows, this witness has been largely in the inward and spiritual realms. Such a situation puts the individual Christian in a special position of responsibility. The Church depends more than ever before on his witnessing to his Master in all the situations and contacts of his daily life. When, in spite of hazards, church membership increases steadily it is an indication of the quality of that witness. The Chinese, we have always known, have their own ways of doing things. Chinese Protestants have chosen the very Chinese way of accepting externally as far as they could and keeping their reservations to themselves. In a recently published Bible study outline the author, an Anglican bishop, goes into the question of how Christians can co-operate with Communists who do not believe in God, and advocates a policy of standing together with the people, because only thus will they be in a position to preach the gospel of Christ to them. This is perhaps a policy of rationalization. It is open to question whether an uncompromising attitude like that of Wang Ming-tao and his followers, with its inevitable consequences, might not in the long run have put the Church in a stronger position. But the way of quiet infiltration by the unobtrusive witness for Christ in words and deeds has proved its worth often before, and if God accepts and uses this kind of witness, what have we to say?

This very independent Chinese Church, though it stresses its continued membership in the worldwide Christian fellowship at the level of prayer, it not over-anxious to re-open contacts with the West and our suggestions in this matter were met with some reserve. Individual Christians were glad to have news of Western friends, they sent greetings back to them, but correspondence did not seem to be generally wanted yet. Several times the suggestion was repudiated that it might be dangerous for them to write or to receive letters from the West, and it was explained that they had not written because they were too busy with reconstruction. They are certainly busy, but the explanation is hardly valid. There is no doubt that during the early campaign to "sever all imperialist connections" letters coming from or written to England or America would have led to questioning of patriotic sincerity, if not indeed to something more serious. Even now, a large number of letters would be an embarrassment, except for the trusted veteran patriot. There *is* a gap in the curtain, however, and if the Quaker Mission did nothing else we hope that we may have helped to widen that gap. The possibility of an interchange of literature came up several times in conversations. The reaction was: "A little would be welcome, but we should not have time to read a great deal." Some of our group had occasion to suggest to two prominent Church leaders the possibility of Chinese participation in international Church conferences. The answer was a cautious "not yet." On another occasion an Anglican bishop expressed his conviction that the time would come soon when Chinese Christians would want to come out "if they can be sure of being accepted as fellow Christians rather than as specimens of some poor persecuted people." The Church in the West can ill afford to continue to be without the fellowship of the Church in China. How long it will be before it is thought right to change the hesitant "not yet" into a joyful "now" will depend not only on the climate of international politics but also on *our* prayers. It is for us to remember that the Universal Church is the Body of Christ and our divisions are His wounds. The healing of these wounds will not be achieved in political conferences but in the hearts and minds of men as they seek to know His will. . . .[6]

Here then we see the reluctance of the Chinese to welcome Western Christian contacts quite concretely expressed. In 1956 Rajah B. Manikam went to China in his capacity of East Asia Secretary for the World Council of Churches, taking with him a letter of greeting and invitation from Dr. Visser 't Hooft. The representative Chinese Christians who talked with the Indian visitor were very cordial in their interest in further contact with India, but did not feel that their priority in interests involved re-establishing relations with the World Council or renewing any relationship with the International Missionary Council, which was seen by them wholly as a missionary structure. The World Council they identify with United States control, because of the declaration at Whitby regarding the aggression on the part of North

Korea, and also there was resentment because it was an ex-missionary who had spoken on the church in China at one of the Evanston meetings, and the Chinese do not feel that such a one can speak for them. As one Chinese replied in the conversation with the Indian visitor, who represented the world church:

> There are three important political elements that we must keep in mind. 1. The distorted picture that missionaries and Western Christians are painting of the Churches in China. 2. Strangely enough, Taiwan is recognized by some as China. Western friends do not understand our feeling regarding Taiwan. It is only the seventh fleet that is keeping Taiwan away from us. 3. Peace. The World Council of Churches' stand on peace is very ambiguous. The Evanston Report says: "We must not seek peace for ourselves but also justice." But peace is most essential to us, and we must strive for peace.
>
> We want to build a new China, and build a new Church in China. That is a big job. Compared with this, Hong Kong and the W.C.C. and I.M.C. seem very insignificant to us. The hostile propaganda against us worries us, but we have learned to ignore it. We cannot spend much time in arguing with others. We must make clear to ourselves how we can be a Christian Church in a Communist China. What is the place of Christian witness in this land? How and why do we support wholeheartedly the Communist Party? These are far more important questions to us than our relationship to the International Missionary Council and the World Council of Churches.[7]

Within the conferences and committee meetings of the World Student Christian Federation, too, there have been times of tension. The Korean Student Christian Movement delegation left the General Committee meeting at Tutsing, when the group of Christian students from the People's Republic of China was recognized as participants, and other WSCF gatherings have seen the withdrawal of the mainland Chinese delegation when one from Taiwan appeared. So within the world-wide Christian community the rift and alienation deepen. More recent contacts with the Chinese church and representative Christians indicate that the welcome to conversation is not yet to be assumed, and in the most recent encounter between Chinese and some members of the Western nations who joined in the Christian Peace Conference at Prague in June of 1961, there was a delegation of Chinese Christians. Their report was presented by Bishop K. H. Ting and a reading of it only serves to underline the continuing resentment against the United States, the withdrawal from an organization such as that of the World Council along with a real openness and warmth for fellow Christians in the Soviet zone, and yet a basic affirmation of belief in the power of the risen Christ and of his Incarnation in a sinful world.

What does all this mean for us? It is here that we are on the real frontier of reconciliation, for we do live in the same world. How can we discover a way of living together, of dealing honestly with each other within the over-arching care of God, who loves us all, Christians of China and of North America, and the people of both lands, who do not yet pledge to our God their allegiance, we who are still his children?

As a Canadian, I have attempted to share what understanding I have gained from both experience and study. When we were being surrounded by hateful words and influences in a China very recently gone Communist, it was easy to meet hate with hate and resentment with bitterness, but these are self-defeating. Love and forgiveness are not flabby things which lead to political appeasement or compromise. But when bitterness blinds us to the lessons that God may have for us to learn, when communism becomes the only enemy, and this leads on to a fear that paralyzes clear thinking, it is very easy within our own society to support policies which are denials of the freedom and the democracy which we prize. The total control and mutual distrust, which seem to me to be the most demonic aspects of an ideology that looks to no authority beyond that of man, may easily come to be accepted in our own society unless we can keep clear heads.

What does this mean? What can it mean? It means first the real discipline of knowing our faith. It means commitment to the point where we begin to act out of faith, not react simply in terms of culture; to make decisions in the light of that faith.

Then as we consider the relationships of today's world, we must listen to our fellow men in Asia and Africa and Latin America and really try to understand their situation. And this may mean long disciplines in appreciation of histories and cultural heritages which are often much deeper and more varied than our own.

With even partial knowledge of Chinese history, and particularly that of the last hundred years, we come to a new appreciation and understanding. The judgments we make can be in terms of China herself, and not just of the relation of China to us. For instance, for how many is the interest in China focused in a fellow-feeling for the Christian church and its program of work in China, so that we center on the concerns of a group which at the largest estimate claimed about 3 per cent of the population of the country. (Of this number 2 per cent were Roman Catholic and 1 per cent Protestant.) Yet our interest in our fellow Christians, right and intimate as it should be, is inevitably distorted if we do not appreciate the whole of the situation in which this tiny minority exists and to which it must witness. So let us at least make an effort to be informed, and with some sense of objectivity.

We need to develop some political realism about the permanence of the People's Republic of China, and as citizens help formulate policies that will solve some of the anomalies of the international scene today.

We will underestimate entirely what is happening in China —and with dangerous consequences—if we cannot acknowledge the positive accomplishments of the People's Republic. With enormous energy and idealism and against great odds the Chinese have set out to construct a modern, industrialized China, and they are understandably proud of their progress.

For God's people in China we can give thanks. But let us not think that if we do this and study China's development and history and values we may assume that Chinese Christians will naturally agree with our conclusions. In the present state of international communication it is evident that we will come out at very different conclusions from those that are convincing for our fellow Christians in China, as they face the realities for their work and witness in the People's Republic of China. We may disagree profoundly and almost certainly will be hurt in the process of trying to listen and understand. Let us be willing to absorb a bit of hurt, and above all to recognize the integrity of these our fellows in their own search for obedience, even when our call to obedience seems so very different. It may well be that God has lessons for his Church which will only be learned in Marxist lands. And this will still be true whether we happen to like it or not. The Church is there in China because of God's grace and power. The Body of Christ, there as here, is in his hands. What is God's word to us in the complexities of a world blighted by alienation in which Christians, God's servant's, find themselves tragically caught; blighted by race discrimination, the imperialist and colonial heritage of oppression and benevolence, ideological confusion, and corruption of power tied to the possibilities of global annihilation?

"The whole creation is on tiptoe to see the wonderful sight of the sons of God coming into their own."[8] So Paul saw the possibilities in his day. What would happen if the avowed servants and sons really could reach their maturity? There is an excitement of expectation in creation itself if we can sense it. Where is our obedience? How do we become the agents of the reconciliation, working in the power of the Great God and Father of our Lord Jesus Christ?

NOTES

PERSPECTIVE

1. There are, of course, other groups of Chinese Christians whose quite different story is also important and has been more frequently told—particularly the Roman Catholics and the evangelical groups, many of whom have been squeezed into the patriotic stream, or out of existence, as the pinchers of a totalitarian ideology tighten on the whole nation.

CHAPTER 1

1. *China Bulletin,* August, 1961. A monthly publication of the Far Eastern Office, Division of Foreign Missions, National Council of Churches of Christ in the U.S.A.
2. Mrs. Lapwood left China in 1952, and the account refers to a return visit of six weeks with her teen-age daughter during the summer of 1960.
3. Lapwood, Nancy H., "China Revisited" *Reconciliation,* May-June, 1961. Published by the Fellowship of Reconciliation, London.

CHAPTER 2

1. *China Bulletin,* March 1, 1954.
2. To gain some depth of understanding here, see *How to Serve God in a Marxist Land* by Karl Barth and Johannes Hamel, New York, Association Press, 1959. Also, *A Christian in East Germany* by Johannes Hamel, New York, Association Press, 1960. Both books give an interior sense of the nature and challenge of Christian witness in "God's beloved East Zone," as Pastor Hamel refers to East Germany today.
3. *International Review of Missions,* October, 1957, p. 416. Quoted by permission of the World Council of Churches Commission on World Mission and Evangelism.
4. *China Bulletin,* February 3, 1958.

CHAPTER 3

1. Clyde, Paul H., *The Far East,* Englewood Cliffs, N. J., Prentice Hall, 1958, p. 354.
2. *China Bulletin,* February 9, 1953.

CHAPTER 4

1. Robert Payne, *Mao Tse-tung,* New York, Henry Schuman, Inc., 1950, p. 226. (Used by permission.)
Author's note: Mao's explanation of "monster": "I meant all the evils—the Japanese, the Kuomintang, the terrible social system." The red flag should not be taken to mean only the Communist flag, for here there is a deliberate confusion between the red flag and the red banner carried by ancient Chinese generals. The Chinese mile or *li* is roughly one third of the English mile.

2. Peter Tang, *Communist China Today,* New York, Frederick A. Praeger, 1957, pp. 34-35.

3. White and Jacoby, *Thunder out of China,* New York, William Sloan Associates, Inc., 1946.

4. Read the story of the intellectuals' struggle for truth and for freedom of speech and thought in those days in Robert Payne's books, *China Awake* and *Forever China.*

5. Han Su-yin, *A Many Splendored Thing,* Boston, Little Brown and Co., 1952, p. 126-127. (Used by permission.)

CHAPTER 5

1. Robert Guillian, a French writer, is among those who take this view.

2. See Amaury de Reincourt, *The Soul of China,* and Tibor Mende, *China and Her Shadow.*

3. de Reincourt, *op. cit.,* p. 80.

4. For those who would like to read further on this topic, the article by Harriet C. Mills, "Thought Reform and Ideological Remolding in China," pp. 71f, in *The Atlantic,* December, 1959, is a very useful reference.

5. From a translation sent to Szechwan shortly after the meeting of the National Committee.

6. Quoted in three issues of the *China Bulletin,* May 11, May 25, and June 8, 1959.

7. Kuo, Ping-chia, *China: New Age and New Outlook,* New York, Alfred A. Knopf, 1956. (Used by permission.)

8. *T'ien Feng,* June 24, 1957. Translated by Frank Price.

9. Paul A. Varg, *Missionaries, Chinese and Diplomats: the American Protestant Missionary Movement in China, 1890-1952,* Princeton, N. J., Princeton University Press, 1958, p. 152-3.

10. *Handbook on People's China,* Peking, Foreign Languages Press, 1957.

11. Russian films and the activities of the Sino-Soviet Friendship Society were beginning to spread knowledge of the USSR.

12. See Francis Price Jones, *The Church in Communist China,* New York, Friendship Press, 1962; also David Paton, *Christian Missions and the Judgement of God,* New York, Friendship Press, 1962.

13. "The Church in China: Failure and Future," *British Weekly,* July 17, 1952.

14. Quoted from a bulletin of the conference of Missionary Societies in Great Britain and Ireland.

15. E. Margaret Kiesow, *China—The Challenge,* London, The Overseas Missions Committee, The Presbyterian Church, England.

16. Quoted in *China Bulletin,* March 29, 1954.

17. Quoted in *China Bulletin,* November 3, 1958.

18. Robert Payne, *op. cit.,* p. 256.

19. Margaret Kiesow, *op. cit.,* p. 29-30.

20. Ting Kuang-hsu served on the staff of the World Student Christian Federation in Geneva. Previous to this work he had been World Missions Secretary of the Canadian Student Christian Movement, and followed this assignment with a period of study in New York. At present he has been elevated as Bishop of the *Sheng Kung-Hui* or Anglican Church in China and is also head of the Nanking Theological Seminary. He has attended Lambeth Conferences on several occasions and has been a delegate from China to the General Committee of the World's Student Christian Federation and more recently to the Christian Peace Conference held at Prague in the summer of 1961. Articles written by him may be found in issues of the *China Bulletin,* August 1953, and in the three issues December 9, 23, 1957, and January 6, 1958. These three issues provide a complete text of his treatment of the theme "Christian Theism." The Chinese-English magazine, *China Reconstructs* of June, 1956, carried an article by the bishop entitled, "Chinese Christians: New Prospects, New Unity."

CHAPTER 6

1. Quoted in *China Bulletin,* October 26, 1959.

2. Summary and quotations from *China Bulletin,* December 21, 1959.

3. F. P. Jones, *op. cit.,* p. 162-163.

4. Jean Woodworth, report prepared for the Y.W.C.A.

5. More recently there is the account of Helen Willis, *Through the Encouragement of the Scriptures.* This unfortunately was not accessible for the preparation of the present study, but is reported by the *China Bulletin* to be very relevant.

6. "Quakers Visit China," Society of Friends East-West Relations Committee and Peace Committee, Friends House, Euston Road, London W.W. 1, 1955, pp. 46-48.

7. From the visit of Bishop Rajah B. Manikam of India, to China, "Interview with Chinese Church Leaders at Peking." March 17, 1956.

8. Romans 8:19, *J. B. Phillips: The New Testament in Modern English,* New York, The Macmillan Co., 1960.

THE FORMAT

TYPE: Times Roman 10 point leaded 2 points

COMPOSITION, PRESS, AND BINDING: Sowers Printing Company, Lebanon, Pennsylvania

COVERS: Affiliated Lithographers, Inc., New York

TYPOGRAPHICAL DESIGN: Margery W. Smith

COVER DESIGN: Barbara Knox